Do You Remember?

Alice Taylor

I was born on a hillside farm in the depths of rural Ireland. On this farm, as on many others all over the country, people worked hard with the most basic tools, and with their beloved horses, to wrest a livelihood from the land. They coped with a world that had yet to hear the buzz of an engine or light up at the touch of a switch. Their own tools were often shared with the whole neighbourhood; work, too, was shared and communal, for those difficult jobs requiring strength and numbers. The women who ran the home and the farmyard were the working wives of their day, contributing hugely to the financial viability of the farm. Even we children had our responsibilities – we too learned how to use and take care of the tools for living and how best to use them. Life was lived at a slower pace, though not less hard-working. But without modern machinery everything took its time. I remember it all with a huge fondness. Our farm, our way of life, is forever grafted onto my mind and soul and heart to be remembered forever.

ALICE TAYLOR'S RECENT BOOKS:
To School through the Fields (special edition)
And Time Stood Still
The Gift of a Garden
For a complete list see www.obrien.ie

Do You Remember?

Alice Taylor

photographs by Emma Byrne

First published 2014 by
Brandon,
an imprint of The O'Brien Press Ltd,
12 Terenure Road East, Rathgar,
Dublin 6, Ireland.
Tel: +353 1 4923333; Fax: +353 1 4922777
E-mail: books@obrien.ie.
Website: www.obrien.ie
Reprinted 2014

ISBN: 978-1-84717-684-4

Photography acknowledgements: With thanks to
Peggy and Myley Byrne for the cover image and page 85
Mogue Curtis and 'Johnny' pages 194 and 199. Mogue Curtis page 200

10 9 8 7 6 5 4 3 2
20 19 18 17 16 15 14
Printed and bound in Poland by Bialostockie Zakłady Graficzne S.A.
The paper in this book is produced using pulp from managed forests.

The O'Brien Press receives financial assistance from

Dedication

For my brother Tim,
who was my inspiration and mentor,
and for the ancestors who kept life flowing
through the veins of rural Ireland

Contents

Introduction

The Memory Butterfly

In a long-forgotten garden at the back of all our minds are the faded flowers of a past season. These memory flowers are rooted into the fabric of our being where they sleep quietly beneath years of living. Then one day you hear a song on the radio or a special piece of music is played. Leafing through a book you come across the line of a poem you learned in school. On a garden visit an evocative scent wafts up your nose. You are searching for something in a drawer and an old photograph taken long ago with a brownie camera falls out.

And suddenly you are in another place. A memory butterfly awakens, gently flutters onto one of those faded flowers and gradually it comes to life. Wisps of memory begin to float around your mind and slowly come together. A faded scene forms and beckons you back to a long-forgotten place. As the vague picture begins to emerge you might turn hesitantly to a friend and tentatively ask, 'Do you remember?', or you might say to a person who has a different memory road, 'Wait till I tell you how we did ...'

As you journey back, it is wonderful to have a travelling companion. Maybe someone who has been there too and remembers, or a visitor to those times, someone new to your remembered way of life. You are on the remembering road and a companion is travelling back with you. Together you begin to fill in the missing bits of the jigsaw and explore long-forgotten things. There is a huge sense of satisfaction as the full picture begins to come alive. Sharing the experience is half the joy of travelling the Do You Remember road. And for those new to these long-gone times, having a guide who was there, who can draw you in as if you too were actually reliving these very experiences, is wonderful.

That is what this book is all about. My wish is to be a companion on your journey to other times and other ways, as I remember my home place, my grandmother's dresser, the tea in the parlour, minding the chickens, or poems we learned at school. Clinging to the inside of all our minds like cream to the inside of a jug are the memories of our earliest years. We never quite forget them.

I hope you enjoy sharing these memories with me and that you relish the journey back along the memory road!

How nice to sit and think awhile
Of little things to make you smile
Of happy things you did in fun
Long ago when you were young
To think of people who were kind
And left a ray of light behind
People who were nice to know
When you were young long time ago
So come and sit with me awhile
And think of things to make us smile.

Chapter 1

The Home Place

It takes a lot of living to make a house a home. The living connects ancestry to posterity, creating a nucleus that supports and strengthens the extended family. Like a tree, families put down roots that give support and stability to extended branches. The home family provides a shelter belt and that sheltering can encompass the extended tribe when life gets stormy.

As we become teenagers and adults, many of us may develop a certain disdain for our parents' way of life and discard many of their ideals. We may even revolt against them or indeed abandon their ways entirely, but as we mature we often discover the wisdom in some of the old ways and that we have something to learn from previous generations. Life has

a strange way of opening our eyes to the value of things we once considered outdated. Seamus Heaney captured it beautifully when he said, 'I learned that my local County Derry [childhood] experience, which I had considered to be archaic and irrelevant to the "modern world", was to be trusted.'

Growing up in a home where eight generations of our family had lived I was made aware at an early age of the far-reaching influence of roots. During my childhood, people whose ancestors had been born in our house came back from all over the world to walk the land that had spawned their ancestors. It matters not whether your home place is a tiny cottage or a grand house its umbilical cord has the same pulling power.

Emigration was always part of Irish life and nowhere more than in the hilly regions of the Cork-Kerry border where I grew up and where wresting a living from the land had never been easy. Emigration was the answer to the problem. Young men from our area went mostly to Oregon and San Francisco, and to Australia, and the girls to Boston, New York and Chicago among other places. Some never came back, but generations later their descendants came to explore their roots. These people had grown up in the shadow of their parents' and grandparents' homeland and wanted to find out more about it. It was important then that the people in the home place gave them time, and that they sat down and told them about their ancestral roots. Sometimes these descendants had waited many years and travelled long distances to walk the fields where their parents or grandparents had played and worked as youngsters. Their parents and grandparents had often sent back hard-earned money to keep their home fires burning and their descendants now wanted to hear the stories of the home place which they had probably heard talked about since they were children.

I was amazed as a youngster to discover that deep in the marrow of human beings lies a strong need to connect with our life source – not unlike the salmon and the geese who each year instinctively travel across the world to come back to the birthing place of their ancestors. The laws of nature are beyond our human understanding.

And so, when the visitors came back to our home place long ago all work on the farm was suspended, which impressed me greatly. It could well have been a sunny day and we might have a field of hay mown and ready to be saved. Usually nothing – simply nothing – took precedence over this in my father's world. After all, this was our bread and butter! But, prompted by my mother who treasured family history, my father put the returning descendants before saving the hay. His action spoke louder than any words. At the time we had an old man working with us who constantly reminded my mother that 'Children have only what they see', and later in life a nun at school told us 'Sound is heard but example thunders' – and it's true! My parents were laying the foundation of deep respect for family. I was very impressed.

These visitors got tea in the parlour and sometimes their unannounced arrival meant that one of us young ones had to run all the way into town, which was almost three miles away, to bring back those little extras that my mother felt were necessary for her guests. Though often these niceties were left untouched and my mother's brown bread was what was most appreciated. If she happened to have one of her homemade apple cakes on hand, this was especially savoured with delight – though my mother's delight that we did not already have her apple cake scoffed was far greater than the visitors' appreciation. Niceties in our house had to be kept under lock and key. The parlour table was set with my mother's best tablecloth. Tablecloths at the time were made of pure linen or damask and had to be hand-washed, starched and ironed, and when one was spread out over the large parlour table it breathed 'special occasion'. Then out came her best china and bone-handled cutlery and the 'loaf sugar', or sugar lumps, also kept securely locked away in her deep press beside the fireplace. All this fuss told us that these were special people who were to be welcomed back to their home place with proper ceremony. These returning emigrants also made us aware that we were simply custodians of our land, guarding it for all generations.

When I, like others, left the shelter of the home I took with me a deep love of my home place, and whenever in later life

I hit a rough patch, my best therapy was to go back and walk those fields or to call a sibling, or a member of the extended family, or an old neighbour and talk over the problem with them. I became very grateful for the influence of my roots, and that included my grandmother, aunts, uncles and neighbours. It takes a whole neighbourhood to rear a child.

A few days after my father's funeral the awareness of place really sank home. I walked with my brother down through the fields that our father had worked all his life to the river where he had fished. His spirit walked with us. We stood and watched the river he had loved and cared for flow silently by. On a regular basis he had checked its water for cattle pollution, making sure that nothing entered it to interfere with its fish or bird life. His belief was: wrong nature and you pay a terrible price. There was healing that day in gazing at the water of the river flowing by; an awareness as well of how transient life is and the timelessness of that river and the land of our ancestors that it flowed through. From them we had inherited not only the land but also an appreciation of the gift of life.

By a strange coincidence, the day I finished this chapter I received the following letter in the post which echoed exactly what I was thinking and it stayed with me for days. Here's a short extract:

> Dear Alice, I must write and let you know how much I've enjoyed your book *Gift of a Garden*. The garden gives so much back. To read about Uncle Jacky and to have the fun

of continuing on his pleasure of gardening in his garden is extra joy. If it was anywhere else it wouldn't feel the same. The feeling of belonging, of ownership, or perhaps not ownership – we tend to take care of what's left to us and perhaps when we are gone a little bit of us remains, as Uncle Jacky still remains.

I was born and raised in Dublin. My mother's parents came from Co Carlow. Her parents moved to Dublin but her grandparents and great-grandparents all came from the one little spot. My great-great-grandparents were stonemasons and I was told they built the house and surrounding walls. My mother holidayed every year when we were young down there and what freedom – and such wonderful people. It left a mark on me. They say it gets into your blood. I'd say it's leaded into my marrow.

I have been very lucky to have been given a chance to buy a part of the land down there and to own the remains of a dry-stone cottage where my grandfather and great-grandfather were born. I feel a piece of land gives off its treasures. It can absorb a lot of us back into the soil, to join others gone before us. There's only four walls and a chimney stack left, but what a wonderful thing to come my way. To walk on the same land that they walked on … I hope you don't mind me writing to you. I feel you may understand the wonder of it all.

The Brook

Alfred Tennyson

…I chatter, chatter, as I flow
To join the brimming river,
For men may come and men may go,
But I go on forever.

I wind about, and in and out,
With here a blossom sailing,
And here and there a lusty trout,
And here and there a grayling.

And here and there a foamy flake
Upon me, as I travel
With many a silvery water-break
Above the golden gravel,

And draw them all along, and flow
To join the brimming river,
For men may come and men may go,
But I go on forever…

Chapter 2

The Woman of the House

The kitchen was the hub of the home. It was the cooking zone, bakery, laundry, dining room and at night a social centre, school room and prayer room. And if my mother had bought a roll of material in Denny Ben's draper's shop in town the previous Sunday to make what she called 'up and down' dresses for us, it became a sewing room – as you can gather from the term 'up and down' we were not exactly icons of fashion! My mother's was the only sewing machine in the townland so other women came to do their sewing in the kitchen as well. When the hosting of the Stations came around it was a temporary chapel and

when valuable eggs had to be hatched it became a hatchery. When the door was open in summer the hens, who were free-range in every sense of the word, felt quite entitled to wander in and help themselves to the crumbs that had fallen from the table. If it was deemed necessary to bring mother pig in to have her young, it became a delivery ward. When it incorporated a settle it could also be turned into a temporary hostel for an unexpected caller. All human and animal life on the farm revolved around the kitchen.

All farm kitchens were more or less the same. As well as being the largest room in the house, it was also the only one heated by the open fire that stretched across one end wall. A long press or dresser for holding ware stood across the other end. Originally – before my time – the floor was mud or cobbled, which was impossible to keep clean, and later concrete or quarry tiles were put down as they were able to withstand all the assaults of family and animal life. The ceiling was of slatted ceiling laths that sometimes, due to darkening by smoke, had to be scrubbed and repainted, and then varnished, turning the artist into an upside-down painter like a kind of Michelangelo! The finish of paint at the time was dull and flat, hence the need for varnish to give it a gloss finish. The lower half of the kitchen wall was cased over with timber, which we called 'the partition', but was in fact wainscotting. This was either stained and varnished, or painted and varnished. The paint was usually cream coloured or a pale green, depending on the taste of the woman of the house. The paint manufacturers at the time were Harringtons, and later Uno. The wall above the wainscotting was distempered. Hall's distemper came in powder form and water was added until it arrived at a creamy consistency that was easy to apply. It had a limited colour range, but some colours were actually quite vibrant. Popular at the time was yellow ochre and my grandmother used this to paint the outside walls of her thatched house.

The recess all around the fire was constantly whitewashed. Every Saturday the black crane was swung forward out of the way and with a large bucket of whitewash and a long-handled whitewashing brush, the 'whitewashing of the hob' took place. The long handle was necessary as the whitewash, which consisted of powdered lime stirred with water into a liquid form, could scorch the hands of the worker. The whitewash was applied to both sides of a black track that was created by years of smoke which remained in the middle of the wall behind the fire and disappeared up the chimney. It was deemed a losing battle to try to eradicate this smoke track, so it remained untouched.

A large kitchen table stretched down one side of the kitchen and usually another slightly smaller one stood at the other side; this smaller table was the stand for two enamel buckets of spring water drawn from the nearby well that were on standby for drinking and making tea. Beside them was an enamel bucket of milk collected from the tank or churn before the rest of the milk was carried off to the creamery early in the morning. This was also the resting place for the large brown cakes wrapped in retired flour bags that stood there to cool after coming out of the hot bastable. These indispensable cloths were the bags in which the flour came home from the mill. They were made of a strong cotton or calico, and once empty were washed and rewashed to remove all traces of embedded flour, and then they were laid on a hedge in the garden to bleach under the sun. They were finally ready to do a second term of duty. The flour bags were known as 'bageens' and were made of excellent quality material, and once they had served their original purpose were put to many uses. They became aprons, pillowcases and sheets, and many other things, and gave long years of service in their reincarnation. Recycling was the name of the game.

In the evening the small table became the school desk as we sat around it to do our lessons. Then my mother covered it with newspapers to absorb ink spills and to avoid calculations and impromptu drawings being made on its white wooden face. The main table was usually covered with an oilcloth, but this smaller one was bare-faced and had to be scrubbed white every week, together with the collection of wooden *súgán* chairs from around the kitchen. In winter they were scrubbed in the kitchen using a bucket of warm water and a scrubbing brush with carbolic soap or a little block of red brick which was a hard dry block made from the dust remaining after the making of red fire bricks; in summer the chairs were carried to a water spout at the end of the yard for scrubbing. These chairs had occasionally to be re-*súgán*ed which was a specialised job, and if the man of the house did not have the required skill the local thatcher came to the rescue. The *súgán* was made of ropes of twisted straw saved from the threshing and these were interwoven to make a comfortable seat. Usually accompanying the chairs to cope with an overflow of sitters was a long timber stool known as the 'form' (or as we pronounced it 'forum'), which could seat four to six people depending on their circumference. The children were seated on a form that was usually lined up between the table and the wall – in there they had their backs to the wall, so if a scuffle broke out they were less likely to topple head first onto the hard floor.

For the annual threshing the two tables were brought into action to seat the *meitheal* of neighbours who gathered to get the harvest in. That night the kitchen became a dancehall when the annual threshing dance was held and hob-nailed boots cracked sparks off the floor as neighbours lined up to do the Siege of Ennis, the Haymaker's Jig and Shoe the Donkey to the beat of a local musician who played on a fiddle or accordion for jigs, reels and sets.

The Station mass, which rotated between the farmhouses in each townland, necessitated a huge clean-up when it came around. Then the kitchen became a chapel. The large kitchen table was hoisted up and had two *súgán* chairs slipped under each end, which raised it up to resemble an altar and make it a comfortable height on which to say Mass. Then it was draped in the best white linen tablecloth of the house and two brass candlesticks were placed at either end. At the far end of it or on a small side table, on another white cloth, was a cup and saucer, spoon, a salt cellar, a sprig of palm and a little white linen finger cloth to dry the hands of the priest. That night the kitchen became a concert venue as the family and neighbours tested their performance skills in an impromptu concert.

When the pig was killed the kitchen became a temporary butcher's shop as the meat was cut up and salted on the tables before being plunged into a barrel of brine in the back kitchen, which was cooler than the kitchen. Before the meat was placed in the brine an egg was put in to test that there was enough salt to preserve the bacon. If the egg stayed afloat it was the go-ahead signal for the meat to go in, and if it sank an indication that more salt was required. The bacon was both fatty and salty, which in today's world would be a nutrition-ist's nightmare; possibly the hard labour that was part of life then counteracted any ill effects. Later the kitchen became a smoke-house as pieces of bacon were hung off iron hooks in the ceiling to be seasoned by the fire while the hams disap-peared up the chimney to be smoked for Christmas.

The most important timepiece in every house hung in the kitchen too and this was the clock that guided all our lives. As well as telling the time, these clocks were also an elegant piece of furniture, with a brass pendulum swinging behind a little glass door at the lower end of its oak or mahogany case. Ours was an eight-day clock that struck on the hour and could be heard all over the house. It had to be wound up once a week and in our house this was done every Saturday night. These clocks had come in from America and my father told us that ours was bought by his mother in a local shop around 1915 for five pounds.

The other important piece of furniture in the kitchen was the radio, which kept us informed of how the world outside our world was carrying on, and on summer Sundays the voice of Micheál O'Hehir brought the excitement of Croke Park into the kitchen. My father was a BBC listener and my mother a Radio Éireann woman, but every afternoon she tuned into the BBC for 'Woman's Hour' and 'Mrs Dale's Diary'. We left school at three o'clock and should have been home through the fields in half an hour, but there were so many distractions on the way that often we had to run across the last few fields to make it in time to listen to Mrs Dale's exploits. Later, before the supper at six forty-five, we gathered around the radio again to listen to 'Dick Barton Special Agent', which filled us with wonder at the exploits of the three detectives, Dick, Snowy and Jock. Later they were replaced by 'The

Archers', a farming family whose method of farming was definitely more sophisticated than ours. 'Paul Temple' was another detective series that we found fascinating, and we listened to every play on both stations. We loved 'Question Time' with Joe Linnane and pitted our brains against each other and the radio teams. 'Take the Floor' with Din Joe had us practising our skill in Irish dancing and 'Around The Fire' with Seán Ó Síocháin was a mixture of songs and music, and we each had our own favourite singers. My father was a news addict and had a thirst to know what was happening all over the world, and he also listened to every weather forecast, which was not surprising as farming was so weather dependent, but his avid listening to the shipping forecast was, in our opinion, a bit outside his need-to-know zone. After all, high seas were pretty far removed from the hills of North Cork. The last programme at night was the 'Irish Hospitals Sweepstake' when Bart Bastable told us 'it makes no difference where you are, you can wish upon a star.'

This radio was kept on a high shelf to keep it safe from little fingers or else it was put on the deep window sill. It was a sizeable piece of solid furniture to which two weighty glass batteries were attached, one of which had to be charged regularly or else the voice inside took a vow of silence. Listening time therefore had to be rationed to avoid over-use of this battery. In order to restore the voice, the battery had to be carried to a garage – but in our case a pub in the nearby

town – where it was plugged into a big apparatus which built up its lost vocal chords, and then we were back in business. If the creamery cart was making its daily journey to town with the milk, the battery was carried along, but if this was not the case the weighty battery had to be borne by hand, which was a tough, muscle-straining exercise.

Usually the only picture to grace the walls of the kitchen was of the Sacred Heart, who kept a paternal eye over all our activities, and after supper each night his hour came when we knelt around him to say the Rosary.

I Remember, I Remember

Thomas Hood

I remember, I remember
The house where I was born
The little window where the sun
Came peeping in at morn;
He never came a wink too soon
Nor brought too long a day;
But now, I often wish the night
Had borne my breath away.

I remember, I remember
The roses, red and white,
The violets, and the lily-cups
Those flowers made of light!
The lilacs where the robin built,
And where my brother set
The laburnum on his birth-day,
The tree is living yet!

I remember, I remember
Where I used to swing,
And thought the air must rush as fresh
To swallows on the wing;

My spirit flew in feathers then
That is so heavy now,
And summer pools could hardly cool
The fever on my brow.

I remember, I remember
The fir trees dark and high;
I used to think their slender tops
Were close against the sky;
It was childish ignorance,
But now 'tis little joy
To know I'm farther off from Heaven
Than when I was a boy.

Chapter 3

The Picture that
Told a Story

Before modern art found its way onto the walls of Irish farmhouses the pictures were mostly of the heavenly variety or at least told a story that did not require mental dexterity to interpret the mind of the artist. Our minds were not challenged by the penetrative skills necessary to interpret what was being said by different shades of grey on canvas; Bacon was something we had for our dinner and a Knuttel face never challenged our concept of facial contours. Many houses had a print from Paul Henry's series 'The Potato Diggers', showing farmers digging the fields or, heads bent, stopping to say the Angelus, and even though they were dressed in a totally different garb to ours, these people were still of our world. But mostly, our walls had holy pictures on show.

My grandmother had agonised faces of unknown saints peering down at us and a flying Jesus disappearing into the clouds of heaven who bore us all in that direction. From the wall above my bed a beautiful Saint Teresa poured a shower of roses down over me. She looked serene and very detached from the hard work of farm life. In her flowing Carmelite habit she projected an image of inner peace and the tranquility of monastic life. This, I decided, was the life for me! No hens to be fed or windows to be cleaned. Besides, would I not look gorgeous in those flowing robes? Days spent meandering in meditation around a walled garden picking roses was an enticing idea. So beguiling was the prospect that one evening at the age of ten I presented myself at the door of our local convent and informed a surprised Reverend Mother that I was ready to join her flock. She gently encouraged me to come back later. Later, somehow, never happened.

Saint Francis was the other icon of our formative years. The fact that we had a saintly cousin in the Franciscans who came annually shedding holy pictures like confetti fostered that interest. The picture of Francis surrounded by our feathered friends added greatly to his appeal.

But one picture stood out from all the others. It was the picture of a familiar face that cast a caring eye over us all. On the wall of almost every farm kitchen – and indeed

town ones as well – was the familiar picture of the Sacred Heart. Each new bride began her life with a new picture. My grandmother gave one to my mother when she got married, and my mother gave one to me when I set up my new home, and a few years ago, when my daughter got married, her mother-in-law gave her the traditional mother-daughter picture, which was a symbolic welcome into the female line of her new family.

Each picture began life with the names of the young couple and the date of their marriage. When and if children arrived, their full baptismal names were added. It gave visitors an instant list of the residents and was also a record for the future. At the base of the picture was the name of the priest who consecrated the house to the Sacred Heart, when he blessed both home and family. Unfortunately, however, one omission was the birth dates, which would have made it a very valuable family record.

The picture itself was of a benign-faced, long-haired Jesus, who smiled gently down on us. He belied the fire-and-thunder image projected of him by the Church at the time. Maybe the women introducing him to their daughter's new home had the right thinking and saw real religion as being all about heart and love. To the right of his smiling face was the message: 'I will bless the house in which the image of My Sacred Heart shall be exposed and honoured', and at the other side: 'I will give peace in their families.' Was it any wonder, then, that the woman of the house wanted this peaceful man on board?

The picture began life as a bright vivid image probably purchased at a mission or in the local shop, where the Sacred Heart, Our Lady and the current Pope rested on high shelves above the general mêlée beneath them. The shopkeeper may have felt that divine intervention from above would improve business. Over the years the glossy picture would become muted and mellowed by smoke from the fire, and in our case by smoke from my father's and the neighbours' pipes too as they sat around the open fire and puffed smoke over all and sundry, including the Sacred Heart. This screen of smoke was swished off him weekly with the swirl of an oil-soaked newspaper. Over the years, however, smoke and family living blended the shiny picture and frame into its surroundings. He became one of us and sometimes the family rosary beads hung off his shoulder. Prayers of desperation were flung at him during exams or at times of crisis. But he was never polluted with the commercialism of our daily lives, and the creamery book and bills were tucked instead into the banisters of the stairs. He was a comforting presence in the midst of family chaos and his picture was part of our lives. Did we expect him to perform miracles? Not really! But a bit like my mother, his image was calming when the going got tough. He was strategically placed to be visible from all corners of the large kitchen and sited as he was on the wall opposite the kitchen window he caught your eye as you walked past on your way home and almost seemed to say: Welcome back, I am still here. He was part of the familiar face of home.

Beneath him was his own little beacon of light, and covering the shelf under the lamp was a little lace or hand-crocheted white cloth that draped down around its edges. Perched on this small shelf was a miniature pot-bellied oil lamp and soaking in the oil was a circular wick up through which the oil was fed into a little burner that had at its side a tiny serrated knob to raise the wick as it burnt down. On top of the lamp, kept in place by little brass pods, was a small, jaunty red globe. The Sacred Heart lamp was filled weekly with oil. Then the globe and burner were removed, a tiny funnel inserted into the neck of the lamp and oil poured gingerly from the oil can used to fill the large household lamps. Great care had to be exercised as this lamp was miniature and an overflow resulted in an undesirable smell of oil around the kitchen. Back in action, it glowed red day and night. It was the eternal flame of the home.

The flowers beneath the Sacred Heart picture told the record of the seasons. At Christmas it glowed with red-berried holly and the first flower to peep above the ground in spring was picked to appear in front of him. He went from snowdrops to daffodils to bluebells, to sprigs of palm on Palm Sunday, to roses, to wild woodbine and so on until he arrived back to holly, which as well as appearing in front of him

A JESUIT PUBLICATION

No. 1.

JANUARY 2013

JANUARY

THE IRISH

MESSENGER

OF THE

SACRED HEART,

Official Organ of the Apostleship of Prayer.

THE 125 YEARS OF SACRED HEART MESSENGER

THY ✦ KINGDOM ✦ COME

IHL

STEREOTYPE.

MESSENGER OFFICE
5, GREAT DENMARK STREET,
DUBLIN.

formed a 'Julius Caesar' wreath around his head. The Sacred Heart picture graced the walls of convents, monasteries and other institutions, but it was essentially the picture of the home.

A little magazine called *The Sacred Heart Messenger*, with a bright red cover to match the lamp brought Jesuit words of wisdom into Irish homes for over eighty years. My grandmother read it, my mother read it and now I read it. Over the years it has brought comfort and enlightenment into homes all over Ireland. People write letters of thanksgiving for favours received from the Sacred Heart – pages are lined with them – so the recipients of the blessings of the Sacred Heart are not an unappreciative lot. Being a gardening enthusiast, one of my favourite articles in it is the monthly gardening instructions from Helen Dillon. And the editorial is always full of food for thought. The Sacred Heart picture of my childhood cast a happy glow throughout our young lives and while his picture may have been evicted out of many homes, the *Messenger* travels on.

A Soft Day

Winifred M Letts

A soft day, thank God!
A wind from the south
With a honey'd mouth;
A scent of drenching leaves,
Briar and beech and lime,
White elderflower and thyme;
And the soaking grass smells sweet,
Crushed by my two bare feet,
While the rain drips,
Drips, drips, drips from the eaves.

A soft day, thank God!
The hills wear a shroud
Of silver cloud;
The web the spider weaves
Is a glittering net;
The woodland path is wet
And the soaking earth smells sweet
Under my two bare feet,
And the rain drips,
Drips, drips, drips from the leaves.

Chapter 4

Don't Call the Doctor

Early on Saturday mornings, when she felt that the need had arisen and before we had a chance to get out of bed to escape, my mother arrived with enamel mugs steaming with abominable, evil-smelling senna pods – the sickly, putrid smell assailed our nostrils as she sailed in the door bearing this concoction. The pods had been immersed in boiling water to draw forth their eradicating propensities. The brew smelt like something that had been fermenting in a bad drain for a long time. The faster you drank it, the better for your state of mind. Yeats once said that too long a suffering makes a stone of the heart, and too long a contemplation of my mother's senna pods definitely played havoc with your state of mind. The prospect of drinking it got worse by the

minute and the cooler you allowed it to become the more disgusting it became. Lady Macbeth's advice held good here: 'If it were done when 'tis done, then 'twere well it were done quickly.' But when, finally, in desperation – and with plenty of gagging – you scoffed it down, that was not the end of the story. Oh no! In actual fact, it was only the beginning. The cleansing process would last a whole day.

On his passage through to his final destination Mr Senna Pods made gigantic efforts to make sure that he moved every obstacle in his way. Our internal organs resisted and the ensuing struggle resulted in a painful, cramping battle, which Mr Senna Pods always won. We might not fall down in the battle, but we certainly doubled over. Having mastered many evictions, Mr Senna Pods proceeded determinedly onwards, carrying his spoils of victory – all day he drove relentlessly towards his triumphant homecoming. When finally he puffed through at journey's end, the awaiting reception committee on the last platform was the humble po. Mr Senna Pods, brandishing the aromas of conquest, shot out with unrelent-ing determination. Our test of endurance was over and all stations back along the line were in pristine condition. A final flushing with cups of sparkling spring water was poured down our throats. We would stand to fight another day. No need to call the doctor!

If we heard on the bush telegraph that the doctor was called to a house we considered it a possibility that the next man on call could well be Mike, the local undertaker. You were in dire straits before you called the doctor. Apart from the fact that money was in short supply, the field of preventive medicine and home cures had first to be explored. So to make sure that we seldom saw the doctor, certain steps were taken to keep all systems up and running.

The first of these steps was a huge concentration on the maintenance of a free-flowing system. The word 'system' might usually be thought to refer to bureaucracy, the government and how the country was run, but in my mother's world it was the map of our internal plumbing. She had her own sat-nav to pinpoint the location of our complaints. Her belief was that if our internal road system was running freely the chances were that all else would be well. Certain procedures were ringfenced into our lives for the maintenance of that system. Preventive medicine was the name of her game. Potholes were filled and road blockages cleared before they got a chance to become major problems. She did not believe in backlogs. My mother had never heard of toxin eradication or colon cleansing, but she was a pioneer in the field.

Senna pods were her principal potion, though my father proclaimed that if we drank plenty of water and went out into the fields and ate haws and sloes, they were much better than any pods. We wished on this occasion that she would listen to my father! He practised what he preached and constantly drank copious amounts of spring water from our own well – and lived into his nineties, having had only one stay in hospital to have an eye cataract removed. (While there, he insisted that we bring in his own well water as he did not trust the hospital water.)

Senna pods were only one of the many flushing methods available for the internal organs and with age you graduated into the world of salts. Salts of varied denominations were available and some seemed more likely to kill you than your complaint! First on the hit-list was Andrew's Liver salts, which was the mildest of all and fizzed up into a frothy bubble that had to be swished back before it stopped fizzing. This washed out your liver. Then came Fynnon's salts, considered capable of swishing around your bones and giving them a new bill of health. Then there were Globar salts which were also given to the *bonhams* (piglets), so at least they shared our suffering. Another was known simply as 'Health Salts', which was a rather vague, innocuous term to cover everything and mean nothing. But Epsom salts were the mainstay of the salts world and were so effective at cleansing the bowel that you felt the tiny granules must have been laced with dynamite! No matter what your complaint, the cure began with a dose of salts.

But a still more disgusting cure of the time awaited us, and that was castor oil. Before we'd got a shot of this, we thought that there could be nothing worse than taking salts. But there was! Castor oil clung like grease to the inside of your mouth and half-blocked your throat on its way to assail whatever it was supposed to assail. My grandmother was a firm believer in it and stood guard at the bedside to make sure that every last drop was dispatched down the throttle. She herself was an advocate of cascara, another frequently used laxative. Each night, having doffed her multi-coloured layers of underwear, she stood inside her bedroom window examining the night sky and sipped her black cascara as if she was enjoying the best of bourbon! If it tasted half as bad as it smelt, it was not a pleasant late-night beverage, but her commentary on the night sky did not falter one syllable as she downed her nightly quota. My grandmother was not a woman to be buckled by something as ordinary as cascara.

Syrup of Figs was the kind small brother of the laxative world and slipped smoothly down your throat leaving a pleasant herbal taste on your tongue. Oh that his big brothers could be as sweet! And if there was any question of the clarity of the output of your urinary system, pearl barley was simmered by the fire and the resulting beverage was sipped under supervision – in case you shared your dose with a convenient cat or dog.

In her old age my grandmother occasionally summoned the doctor, but it had more to do with using him as a sounding board than wanting him to investigate the state of her health. She invariably questioned his diagnosis, to his immense frustration. But she cured herself. When her back gave trouble she had 'the red plaster', which was perforated with holes and lined with a sticky black pad; this clung to her back and was left in place for a long time. If her chest was giving trouble, she had a red flannel that she used as a body warmer to ease her congestion. She was a great believer in Sloan's Liniment and as she applied it the entire bedroom filled with its strong smell – I found it strangely intoxicating and I think that it might have been possible to have a high on the smell. Goose grease for joint lubrication was another one of her aids to flexibility. The fact that goose grease was massaged into unyielding boot and horse leather to make it more pliable could have something to do with the belief in this cure.

Food, too, was used to cure. My mother sent us out to gather crab apples, which she stewed slowly in a pot over the fire. While the crabs stewed, she bridged the backs of two chairs with the handle of a brush. Then she poured the contents of the pot into a muslin sheet that she gathered into a little bag, tied with a firm knot, and hung off the brush handle. The liquid dripped into an enamel bucket until all that was left was the apple debris, which was fed to the pig; pigs loved it – they enjoyed apples anyway and often broke into the orchard to scoff the windfalls, much to my mother's annoyance as these could be used to make apple jelly. When the ditches were strewn with blackberry laden briars, full of vitamin C, we were sent out with tin gallons to pick them for jam.

Carrigeen moss, found at the seaside, smelt like cat's pee. It was simmered for long periods and the offending liquid was then drunk. It had a revolting taste, but if lemons were available a squirt of lemon greatly improved the flavour. But, lemons or not, we had to force it down because it was deemed to have health-giving properties. Later we discovered that carrigeen could be poured into a mould, allowed to set, and with different flavours added could be quite edible. But I could never quite forgot that smell of cat's pee! And when we went to Ballybunion on our summer holidays we were sent out to gather seaweed off the black rocks, and this was taken home to be eaten over the winter as a tonic. It had a fishy, sea-water taste and got stuck between our teeth. My grandmother assured us that it was full of iodine and very good for us.

The local chemist, who was a man for all ills, sometimes came into our orbit. Bottles of iodine were purchased there and used on cuts and bruises as a protection against infection. It also stung like a wasp and caused the recipient to dance a jig of agony around the kitchen until the raw pain of the application subsided. Peroxide, which was a gentler healer and cleanser, was sometimes applied and when it touched the cut formed a frothy cleansing fizz, and as the fizz ceased the pain eased. Sometimes a poultice of hot bran, white bread or flax seeds was placed on pink lint fabric and applied to a wound to draw out infection. The hotter the better! And the hotter the poultice, the louder the tortured shouts of the recipient.

Once I got ringworm from the calves, which was not an uncommon happening as ringworm was very contagious. The chemist covered it with a smear of a black tar-like substance. For a couple of hours after the application the pain was so bad that I considered it a strong possibility it was going to kill me, whereas I had never heard of anyone dying from ringworm. However, it was the ringworm that died, and I survived.

The main disinfectants used in the house and farm were Jeyes Fluid, sheep dip, Lysol, and Scrubbs Ammonia, and all were instantly identifiable by their different aromas, some of which were simply dreadful. A whiff of undiluted ammonia could almost knock you out. Washing-soda crystals soaked in hot water was an all-round cleanser and disinfectant used for outhouses and sheds. Before use, all of these disinfectants were diluted in buckets of water and swirled around with the aid of a stick to avoid skin contact as they were not kind to hands. Rubber and plastic gloves had yet to come on the market. Dried lime, known as slaked lime, was scattered around farm sheds to keep them bug free and the danger here was of a particle blowing into your eye.

But the great fallback for all occasions was the carbolic soap that came into action in the wash tub, and was used for washing floors and furniture, and indeed for medicinal purposes as well. When other poultices failed, carbolic soap laced with sugar and rolled out flat to apply as a poultice, was sure to do the job. It was also a cure for the bad, oily skin of pimply teenagers, and in this case, too, buttermilk was deemed a good cleanser.

Our old helper, Dan, declared mature buttermilk to be a great cure for a hangover and also a wonderful soother for a bad stomach. He also had great faith in the power of a bowl of black porter into which a red-hot iron poker was plunged, declaring it to be full of vitamins – but it had to be a pure iron poker, not a 'modern fandangle', as Dan called it. When he performed this operation, the mulled porter frothed up and filled the kitchen with a heady, brewery-like smell. Sometimes he added a shake of brown sugar to improve the flavour. When my mother was not looking we got a sip, and it was gorgeous. Dan also had great faith in the healing properties of fresh hot cow dung in spring when it was rich in herbs processed in the cow's stomach. My grand-mother agreed with him in this, and when my sister got a dog bite that was difficult to heal, she proved her point by curing the wound with this substance.

Onions were in constant use as deterrents of colds. They were boiled in milk and then the hot milk drunk, mostly at bedtime when it encouraged a restful night. And a piece of heated onion, wrapped in cotton wool and soaked in warm olive oil, was eased into aching ears to heal and soothe

the pain. Then, too, we grew many breeds of cabbage, but kale was regarded as the king of the crop for health-giving properties.

Dandelions, which we children called piss-a-beds, were in fact diuretics, so we were not far off the mark. These were mixed through salads and scrambled eggs to improve personal plumbing. We also ate the leaves of the whitethorn and sorrel leaves, which we called 'sour leaves', and, of course, the haw and the sloe, which were my father's mainstay. We sucked the bells of the wild fuchsia, making sure beforehand that a honey bee was not in residence. All these foods were deemed good for our health and cleansing of body or blood – I'm not too sure which!

Honey was regarded as the king of health-giving properties. An uncle of ours kept bees in straw skeps, but when my brother acquired a swarm he invested in a hive, and from then on we had a plentiful supply of honey. First it was comb honey, which took pride of place on the breakfast table, and we scooped the honey off the comb with a spoon. Then he progressed to an extractor and jars of honey joined the comb. The hives increased and our honey production overflowed into local shops and even further afield.

Nettles, of course, were served three times in the year to improve the condition of our blood, and rhubarb, known in Irish as *purgóid na manac* ('the purgative of the monks') did the same for us.

Our first experience of white-coat medicine was the visit
of the school dentist, and oh boy did she turn our school
into a chamber of horrors! It was the era of 'out with everything' with no prior consultation – anything showing signs
of trouble was simply whipped out. There was no such thing
as fillings. A large, formidable woman, reeking of disinfectant, she arrived wearing a crisp white coat and wielding
instruments of torture. Because we had no running water
or heating system, she had brought along her own equip-
ment, which included a primus stove and methylated spirits.
As she prepared for action, our chalk-smelling room took
on the whiff of a torture theatre. But we were too innocent
and naïve at first to know what was coming down the track.
Unsuspecting, we were lined up like lambs to the slaughter
and Mrs Hitler mercilessly dug teeth from the depths of our
jaws and cast them into a blood-spattered enamel bucket
beside us. The school filled with terrified screams and we
were dispatched home with swollen jaws and blood-filled
mouths. It was not a pleasant introduction to the world of
dentistry!

Compared to Mrs Hitler, Mr Senna Pods had been a walk
in the woods. Well, almost!

Chapter 5

The Long Litany

For many years Lord Nelson dominated the main street of our capital city, but one night he made a surprise guest appearance at our family rosary. Though not of our persuasion, we were nevertheless delighted to welcome him – this was long before some of our less tolerant brethren decided to blast him into oblivion!

My mother's rosary beads were black and battered. They swung off a knob on the shutter of the kitchen window. Black thread, used for emergency repairs, sprouted here and there like black spiders between the decades. These beads were made of cow horn, and from daily use over the years the smaller beads were well rounded, while the large ones, denoting a change of decade, had developed a hollow in the middle, which with

time had acquired the appearance of tiny black boats. These beads were the bridge that linked my mother's everyday world to an unknown spiritual region. From that rich, hidden world she drew strength to cope with her daily routines.

My mother's God was kind and helpful. She had probably decided that her life was sufficiently challenging without entertaining a harsh creator. Not for her the cold, unyielding God of the time, but rather a kind-hearted, understanding God who listened to her problems. She also considered him to be smart enough to listen to the counsel of his own mother, and my mother was determined to have the ear of his mother. So every night she brought her unruly brood and anyone else who happened to be present to their knees around the kitchen. This was her attempt to introduce peace and quiet and law and order into the normal mayhem that prevailed in her corner of the world. It was her time with her God and she wanted her children to be part of it.

Through a wise and sensitive interpretation of the religious practices of the time she had created her own deep spiritual foundation that enriched the demanding lifestyle of her time. She judged her God to be understanding, and her fellow human beings to be as good as they could be, and if they were ever found wanting she deemed such weaknesses to be outside their remit. My father, while taking a benign view of her angle on God, was in strong disagreement with her view of her fellow human beings: he never expected too much from them and was always prepared for the worst, and he informed us that you could never really know anybody until you had either land or money dealings with them.

While my mother's rosary beads were the same throughout the years, my father's were constantly getting lost, or in the wrong pocket, which often reduced him to counting the prayers on his fingers and telling us that 'fingers were there before beads'. He cracked his knuckles as he counted out the decades. Children did not have rosary beads – they were usually acquired as a gift at Confirmation, so we too used our fingers. One felt that my father endured rather than enjoyed my mother's rosary. But he knelt obediently like the rest of us while she launched into 'Oh Lord, thou wilt open my lips' and we all chimed back 'And my tongue shall announce Thy praise.' Then she instructed 'Incline unto my aid, oh God' and we extended the instruction 'Oh Lord make haste to help us.' After that came the Glory be to the Father, which she followed with the 'I believe in God', and we all joined in for the last few lines. Then came the Our Father, three Hail Marys and the Glory. All this before the rosary even began! Then we were finally ready for the decades. We each knew the decade we were to give out and, like well-trained athletes in a relay race, we always picked up at the right place. All this went according to plan with no variation until my mother finished the final Hail Holy Queen – then she could run into trouble as the time came for some creativity and invention.

She usually began one of her long litanies, in which she cajoled an amazing number of heavenly bodies, including the gates of heaven, to come to our aid. One night she got lost in these heavenly regions and could not get her bearings. She continued to circle around these celestial heights with no acceptable signposts in sight and no landing bay coming to her rescue. Eventually, one of my less helpful sisters prompted, 'Try Nelson's Pillar.' This suggestion was met by an unedifying outburst of laughter from around the kitchen. When the hilarity continued without restraint, my father came to my mother's rescue and quelled the disturbance by his usual method – using his cap as a flying missile at the offender. On that particular night, because law and order had broken down completely, he had to launch several scud missiles before peace was eventually restored.

Then came prayers for needy neighbours and relatives gone on roads less desirably travelled, leading us on to an array of other requests until we eventually finished up in Russia, praying for its conversion. My mother's prayers were not confined to the welfare of her own state.

Finally my father had enough and when a few restless coughs failed to have the desired result he became more vocal and declared, 'Missus, we'll be here until morning.' My mother's name was Lena, but when she was driving my father beyond the limits of his endurance she became 'Missus'. We knew then that the end was in view and that we would soon be up off our knees. She always concluded with the Memorare, then there were always a few moments for silent prayer when each one of us was given time to communicate whatever we wished with whoever we thought might be listening.

Sometimes a bit of scuffling for chair possession could take place during the rosary as some of us endeavoured to flex our muscles and evict a sibling who we felt was grabbing more than their rightful share of kneeling space. We were scattered around the kitchen kneeling against *súgán* chairs or timber stools or against the front window sill. This haphazard arrangement evolved nightly and commenced with my father removing his cap and placing it on the floor by his chair. The removal of my father's cap was a rare event and only happened in church or for the rosary – God was the only man for whom my father doffed his cap and bared his head! Once he was in position, we each found a place around the kitchen, kneeling in front of a chair or side-on to a chair. Nobody had a fixed place but went wherever the spirit moved us. Sometimes this could lead to a struggle for possession and my mother would wait patiently until all squatters' rights were established. However, she might not be out of trouble yet as during the recital of the rosary a fit of giggling could break out when some budding comedian decided to make funny faces at the most easily distracted, or do a comic act and trigger waves of suppressed laughter. My mother waited patiently for law and order to return, but if it took longer than my father deemed necessary

his usual missile came whizzing across the kitchen and clipped the ear of the most obvious culprit, and order was restored.

In the summer the front window was my favourite kneeling location because, as well as being out of the normal combat zone, I could look down over the fields and watch the cows lying down chewing the cud or grazing peacefully. Sometimes the young calves ran around an adjacent field and the horses, after their day's work, grazed in their own field, known as *páirc na gcapall*. In the distance the changing evening light on the Kerry mountains made one aware that the gates of heaven could be found in many places.

Over the years I have always been grateful to my mother for her nightly practice of the rosary. At the end of the day it brought us all together in some fashion or other, and allowed silence to descend on our often noisy household. There was a sense of togetherness as we all knelt around the kitchen, and later when I left home it was always comforting to know that I was included every night in her rosary. The mantra of her rosary, learnt in our old farmhouse, has seeped through my life and resurfaces like a calming hand when the waves are high. In later life I also discovered that when death made an unexpected visit the repetitive format of the rosary was the mantra that calmed chaos and induced peace into shocked minds. Recently, when my brother died in our old home, his son knelt at his wake and led us all in the rosary. I remembered my mother with gratitude.

Chapter 6

Always on a Sunday

The first question in our penny catechism was: 'Who made the world?' And the answer was: 'God made the world.' To my seven-year-old mind the world was a pretty awe-inspiring place, filled with wonder and delight. I loved to look out the window at night and see the moon shine on the shadowy fields of cows and light up the faraway Kerry mountains on the horizon. It was blissful to feel the warm grass beneath my bare feet and sense, rather than know, that the same sun turned green shoots into golden grain. Watching calves gallop down a sunlit field in the exultation of their first taste of freedom was a delight. God had created all these wonders, I learned, and had created me too – with some help from my father and mother, though I had yet to figure that one out. So the natural assumption was that if God made all of this, he must be pretty impressive, a force to be reckoned with.

So it should have followed naturally that nurtured by a God-fearing mother, a catechism-teaching school, with a Church permanently hovering in the background, that I would automatically accept all that I was taught without question. This did not happen, however, because my father balanced the whole equation with a healthy cynicism towards the prevailing culture. Some of the Church practices of the time he declared to be crazy, and constantly told us that no Church was more correct than another. If God was smart enough to create the world, and my father had no reason to think otherwise, then there was no way that this God would dream up some of the rules and regulations that our Church had dreamt up, he stated. He regularly proclaimed that the only laws God gave us were the Ten Commandments, and that if the powers that be had been smart enough to have left it at that, our world would be far less complicated.

Despite all these proclamations, every Sunday morning he tackled up the pony and trap and carted us all off to Mass. You would have thought that with his critical attitude to the Church he would have been the one to be late and my mother the one to be rushing out the door in a hurry to get there in time. But the direct opposite was in fact the case. He took very seriously the third commandment, which

instructed us to 'keep holy the Sabbath day'. Once the cows were milked on Sunday morning he turned off his working mind. Instead of working, he went fishing. He felt that, apart from religious considerations, we all needed a break. It was only in a very wet summer that he would entertain saving the hay on a Sunday.

At Sunday breakfast he would regale us with stories of his youth and it was the only time that I ever remember my father singing – he would tilt back his chair and chant out 'The Old Bog Road'. He was not a singer, so 'chant' is as good a word as any to describe the rendition. Then he would turn on the BBC, of which he was a faithful fan, and tell us to listen to the Church of England service as they were telling us the same story we would be hearing later from our own crowd.

After breakfast the ritual of the cut-throat razor came into play. The name of this lethal weapon describes it perfectly. Out came his shaving bowl from behind a dish in the press. Earthenware and shaped like a chalice, it was filled with tepid water, and with the combination of a stick of shaving soap and a shaving brush he worked up a soapy lather that was then transferred to his face – and then the cut-throat was wielded. One false move and you could inflict a fatal wound, but from years of practice he could steer it safely around all the contours and corners of his face. While this operation was in progress the surrounding floor took on the appearance of a snowy field, which he took for granted one of us children would clean up, much to our annoyance.

Then he disappeared upstairs to return shortly afterwards in his Sunday suit and best cap. He then sat on the bottom step of the stairs and eased on his soft leather boots. My father never wore shoes. Neither did he ever polish his own boots, but then neither did any one else in the house. We had a resident shoe polisher – and that was me! We all had our own jobs – there were the inside jobs and the outside ones, the daily ones and the weekly ones, and I hated them all. I felt that life would be a doddle if there were no jobs. But my father firmly believed that unless you learned to work before you were sixteen years of age, you were useless for life. As well as that, there was no one else to do the jobs, so jobs were part of our way of life. The daily outside jobs consisted of feeding the hens, pigs and calves, bringing in the cows and, for the older ones, milking. The daily inside jobs were washing the ware, brushing the floor and setting the table. We usually worked in pairs, an older and younger sister. The jobs rotated, but some weekly ones remained fixed, and that was how every Saturday evening I finished up polishing all the shoes. I sat on the bottom step of the stairs and laid a newspaper on the floor, and, with a knife that had lost its head, scraped all the shoes clean. Then I polished and shone them, and when I lined them all up in a row, from the smallest to the biggest, there was a certain satisfaction of a job well done. I was as pleased as Punch with myself. Maybe my father had a certain grasp of child psychology for which he never got credit!

Once he had his boots on, my father was ready for Mass – but he was the only one. He had five daughters and he complained constantly that he spent his whole life waiting for women! But of all of us, my mother was by far the worst culprit in running late. While he waited for her to come downstairs he got madder and madder, until finally he yelled up the stairs, 'Missus, are we going to Mass today or next Sunday?' My mother would eventually arrive unfazed, pulling on her hat and stuffing odds and ends into her handbag. We all climbed into the trap and the pony took off up the passageway to the road. In summer this was a lovely trip, but in winter you could be frozen stiff or drenched wet, depending on prevailing weather conditions. If the road was icy there was the additional hazard that the pony might slip and we would all tumble head-first out onto the road.

When we arrived in town we went into the backyard of Denny Ben's draper's shop where the pony, along with a few others, was tied up under a tree until his passengers returned. We all headed for the church, but went in different doors: there was the men's aisle and the women's aisle; but the three galleries, including the choir gallery, were mixed. The main long aisle straight down in front of the altar was known as the men's aisle, and originally it was mostly men, but many men felt that the back porch was as far as they could go, and if an over-zealous priest tried to remedy that situation he was left talking to vacant spaces. How all this segregation evolved I have no idea, but that was the way it was. We children went into a side aisle, which was a women's aisle, with my mother, and men did not venture in there. We could see the people in the gallery across the way, which was mixed, and because women at the time wore hats to Mass, the wide variation of head gear made for interesting viewing. If any out-of-the-ordinary outfit appeared, you knew that somebody had got a parcel from America.

The Mass was said in Latin, with the choir chanting down from the choir gallery. The sermons varied from bad to good and sometimes very good. The ringing of the bell in preparation for the Consecration spread a sense of anticipation through the congregation and during the Consecration you could hear a pin drop in the church. This filled me with a sense of wonder that something beyond my understanding was taking place – later in my catechism I came across the word 'transubstantiation' and decided that some things were indeed beyond explanation. But the feeling that something mysterious was happening remains with me to this day.

After Mass there was no talking in the church, but once outside the door my mother met up with women from around the parish and long chats took place, while rows of men assembled outside the church gate to discuss parish and farming affairs. From there the men retreated to the corner of the street or to the local pubs to continue their conversations. We always called into an aunt's house for tea and apple tart, and then went down town where my mother did her weekly shopping. Denny Ben had a great draper's shop and he sold everything, from underwear to outerwear for men, women and children. You could be togged out there for hail, rain, snow or sun. He had huge rolls of material for the making of coats, dresses and all kinds of everything. During purchases in this shop, Denny Ben and my mother had long conversations tracing relations and family history, not alone of both their families but of the entire parish. Denny Ben knew the whole parish and the whole parish knew Denny Ben. Sometimes, as a result of material bought here, a trip to the dressmaker was included if my mother was getting a new coat or costume, or if one of us was getting a new coat. But this was rare as it was the era of hand-me-downs, so one coat could have many reincarnations: let down, turned up and finally turned inside out. We got value out of our clothes!

When my mother had all that she needed she retreated to Mrs Cronin's butcher's shop at the end of the town where a long consultation was held before any purchase took place. 'Fresh meat', as we called, it was a rarity and a great luxury in our house as we killed our own pigs and chickens and they were the staple diet. While this exchange was taking place we went into the kitchen and sat by Mrs Cronin's range.

Finally, when my mother was ready, one of us was sent to the pub to round up my father, and if we were lucky one of his friends came good with a 'stand' – a gift of money slipped into our hand – which could be anything from a penny to a sixpenny bit, and wonder of wonders you might strike oil and get a two-shilling piece!

Then we headed for home and if along the way we passed a neighbour that my mother deemed needed a lift, one of us would be unloaded unceremoniously and left to walk. The walker, whose progress was as fast as the pony as he was now pulling uphill, had the job of opening all the seven gates on the passageway down to our house. This prevented the arguing that usually went on as to who would get out of the trap to open the gates. All these gates were necessary to keep the animals segregated in the different fields.

Once home we had what my mother termed a 'tea dinner', which consisted of cold meats, and a Sunday treat of sweet cake or sometimes a Swiss roll. Then we had jelly and custard, or jelly and cream skimmed off the tank of milk. There was no big cook-up on Sunday. After all, we were having a day of rest and in our house that included the woman of the house.

Chapter 7

The Sewing Box

'Oh the sewing machine, the sewing machine

A girl's best friend

If I didn't have my sewing machine

I'd a-come to no good end ...'

This song, belted out by Betty Hutton on our radio, did not have a musical backing but instead had the insistent rhythm of a fast-moving sewing machine. We recognised it immediately because my mother's sewing machine, which held us all together, made the same sound when she put it into top gear. She and my grandmother made all our clothes. Every draper's shop had shelves of material and knitting wool, but Denny Ben's was to us the Aladdin's cave of

them all. Huge rolls of material lined his high shelves and he would climb up a tall stepladder to lift one down, then land it with a thump on his wide, wooden counter. He rolled it out with a flourish and folds of material poured out along the counter and down the sides. It was lovely to sniff the different aromas that breathed the story of their journey. A brass measuring tape attached to his side of the counter was used to measure out the required amount.

My mother bought yards of grey flannel to make the skirts of our warm petticoats, and white flannelette that was more pliable for the tops. There was a great need for warm underwear as there was no heating around the house and the school was like an ice-box. The only answer was layers of warm clothing. Denny Ben had large cardboard boxes of vests and knickers made of wool and interlock. These garments were the first to be donned in the morning when, with chattering teeth, we jumped out from under the warm blankets onto a cold linoleum floor in sub-zero temperatures. The vest had long sleeves and the warm, ample knickers that encompassed us from waist to knee cap were elasticised around the waist and above the knee. They were either pink or blue, which gave rise to the colour term 'knickers pink'. Before your petticoat was donned, you put on what was known as a bodice, which was made of interlock material and fitted around your top half. The knickers took care of keeping the lower region warm. Then you put on the petticoat, followed by the outer garments. Material was bought to make skirts or pinafore frocks, as we called them – these were simply sleeveless dresses and went on over a jumper or blouse. Long black wool stockings that reached well up under the legs of our knickers were secured in position with a good firm pair of garters and the knickers legs came down over them. This kept cold north winds from circulating in that zone!

In Denny Ben's we also got our strong black leather boys' boots, which were the only ones that would survive the journey across the fields to school. But before we took off in a new pair, my father secured them further with steel toe and heel tips. Over all this ensemble went a long winter coat which was never new. The school coat had always gone to Mass for years, and maybe to school as well on an older sister, and was usually in the last stages of its life. As I've mentioned, 'hand-me-downs' were very commen and it was not unusual to hear the question: 'Is that your own or a hand-me-down?' On top of all this went a rain-hat to act as a water sluice in the bad weather. Sometimes a parcel from America brought a splash of colour, but this was usually for summer wear.

Summer opened a door into a whole new world. Off went all the layers. We could not wait to get rid of them, but my mother believed in: ne'er cast a clout till May is out. But eventually we broke loose, flung the long black stockings and boots under the bed and jumped into light summer dresses. We called these the 'up and down' dresses that my mother had run up on her sewing machine: simply holes for our head and arms, and a run of the machine up and down the sides, and we were ready to go! There was great sense of freedom in being barefoot. On the way to school, early-morning dew ran down our legs, and we raced through muddy gaps and jumped into hot cow dung. It was our early-morning reflexology! Coming home in the evening, we paddled in the streams that divided the fields and tentatively poked our big toe under early frog spawn and in the river felt tiny collies dart around our toes. The journey back and forth to school was a learning curve and an adventure.

A neighbour knit our jumpers. In our townland there were great knitters who constantly sat with clicking needles and delighted in the challenges of cable and diamond patterns and the intricacies of fair-isle. They could knit and chat at the same time, never feeling the need to check on what their hands were doing with the needles. When I tried to learn how to knit in school I became very impressed by their talent – this knitting skill that I had taken completely for granted all of a sudden had turned into a huge challenge. How could these women, whom I had never considered other than ordinary, have mastered this mysterious and difficult art? All of a sudden they became super-women in my eyes.

Our unfortunate teacher grappled with the sticky fingers of a row of ten-year-olds striving desperately to get wool under, over and around hard, sharp steel needles that simply refused to be in the right place. Stitches fell off the needle and holes appeared and endless repetitions finished up in an unrecognisable tangle. Plain and purl that were supposed to produce a neat, even row could turn into a complete mess and have to be unravelled. The first day I encountered these challenges I looked at a knitting neighbour with a new-found respect.

Eventually, when her pupils had mastered the art of one plain, one purl, the teacher tackled the complicated business of turning the heel and closing the toe. This was almost a step too far for me. I watched in awe as our neighbour sped through pairs of socks and added the amazing skills of knitting gloves. She was delighted to help me and we spent hours unravelling – literally – the mysteries of heel-turning and toe-closing. Then, a woman who had married into the next farm did beautiful crochet and embroidery simply while she waited for the dinner to cook! I thought this was just wonderful and I was full of admiration.

As well as knitting, sewing was also on the agenda at school, and in a tall press, or *cófra*, at the corner of the room, our sewing boxes were stacked. They were mostly tin boxes as it was not unknown for a rat to have a late-night supper of a sewing sample, and the place was a race track for mice. So, tin boxes with pictures of curly-haired little girls in frilly dresses running through rose-filled gardens, or with elegant

Edwardian ladies draped across their covers were lifted down once a week for the sewing class. Those covers portrayed a world as far removed from ours as the man in the moon. But it was the contents not the covers that fascinated us.

Each box had a sewing and darning needle, maybe two reels of thread, a thimble, the piece of material on which you were working, and, if you were lucky, an already finished sample of your skill. We learnt tacking, hem stitching, top-sewing and 'run and fell' – and for the life of me I now have no idea what 'run and fell' was all about. It sounds like a cross-country race! Having mastered the various stitches, the next high jump was to do a buttonhole. This was complicated territory, but with much trial and error we got there. Then, for some extraordinary reason, we tackled the complicated business of making a pair of knickers. My mother bought a lovely little piece of cotton adorned with playing children in Denny Ben's for me to make mine. I loved the children playing, but from the start they were destined never to get out to play. Somewhere along the way the necessity of a gusset for leg flexibility was omitted. The children never got out of the box and years afterwards I discovered them in my mother's attic.

One of the problems of the sewing class was the maintenance of a clean 'sewing piece', as it was called. We had no water in which to wash our hands that could have been engaged in easing small stones from between our toes, picking blackberries or making daisy chains. So the miracle was that the sewing sample, on completion, was even recognisable as such.

But of all the skills we learned in the sewing class, the one that I really enjoyed was darning. There was something very satisfying in drawing threads across a large hole with matching wool, and then cross-darning them until the hole disappeared. My mother sat for hours at night by the fire darning socks and jumpers, and when she folded the darned garments she always had about her a great sense of satisfaction.

Chapter 8

Around the Fire

D o you remember ABC? No, I am not talking about the alphabet that opened the door into the written world, but the dark network of fishnet squares that you got imprinted on the front of pale legs if you sat too long and too close to the open fire. But even if it did give us ABC, the open fire was the magnet that drew us all into its embrace. And it was a multi-tasker! It was the cooker, the home heater, the social centre and the comforter for the entire family. It did duty twenty-four hours a day, seven days a week, for fifty-two weeks of the year. It was the focal point of the kitchen and, in winter, of the whole house. Everyone who came in pulled up a chair and warmed themselves in its comforting glow and it could encompass a wide circle as it

stretched across one whole side of the kitchen. And even if you sat alone beside it, you still had company as it told you stories revealed in pictures between the logs and sods of turf. A fire is good company. It was also a constant, moving, living centre around which entire families lived, loved, were educated, read, fought and grew up.

The fire was seen as the heart of the home that never went out and this was probably how a certain old tradition evolved: when entire families emigrated, rather than let their home fire go out the embers were taken across the fields in a bucket or on a shovel to a neighbour's house, where they would continue to glow. In this way, it was felt that the heart of the home would not stop beating and that one day some of the family might return and that once again their own home fire would glow. It probably eased the pain of emigration which, at the time, was often forever.

Built into one corner of the original fireplace was a little corner seat called the hob. This was literally the hot seat as it was so close to the fire it often had to be abandoned by a sweating occupant late at night when the fire grew too hot for comfort. Beside and above it was a small, deep, square recess known as 'the hole', which was used to house the tea caddy, matches and sometimes the pipe of the man of the house. At the other side of the fire was the bellows, which was the heat controller. From beneath the bellows, through an underground tunnel into the ash hole underneath the fire, the bellows whipped air along and caused the fire to dance to its tune. The bellows wheel was iron, and was kept in balance by means of a leather strap that connected it to a lesser wheel, which accelerated the movement of air along the tunnel. It was a simple but very effective device, except when the bellows went out of balance and the strap began to slip off, which sorely tried the patience of the bellows winder. This sometimes required my father – much to his annoyance – to do some necessary adjustments. Eventually the required delicate balance was achieved again and harmony restored to the bellows, the winder, and also to our 'Johnny Fix It', who was not a man of endless patience. Sometimes, if the bellows decided not to cooperate, he swore at it in unrepeatable adjectives!

Beneath the fire the deep ash hole had to be emptied each morning prior to the setting up of the fire for the day. The previous night the *gríosach,* or hot cinders, had been moved to the sides of the grate to avoid being fanned by the air from the ash hole. These hot cinders were clamped down by means of hot ashes that had smouldered slowly overnight, keeping the fire on stand-by.

Come morning, the *gríosach* was hopefully still smouldering. The iron cover was removed from over the ash hole with the long tongs – this cover was perforated with holes to allow the air up from below and the ashes to go down from above into the hole underneath. Sometimes the cover required a visit to the blacksmith to keep it in working order and he also provided replacements if it lost its efficiency due to old age and too much of the fire accompanied the exiting ashes.

This hole was emptied with a tin ponnie or old chipped mug no longer respectable enough for table use. Careful manoeuvring of this mug was needed to avoid burnt fingers from the still-hot sides of the ash hole. Then the cover was replaced and dead cinders put over it to form a bed on which the hot *gríosach* was then piled, and surrounded by little bits of screwed-up newspaper, if available, and light dry sticks known as *cipíní* and soft dry bits of turf. Sometimes, if any of these were in short supply, fine dry hay from the barn was gently introduced. If there was difficulty in getting the flame started, the scarce and valuable matches might have to be brought into action to light the paper or hay. Gentle turning of the bellows slowly coaxed the smouldering flame into life and the fire was gradually fanned into a glow that slowly grew into a strong flame.

I loved the smell of burning hay that turned into a galaxy of blue, yellow and red colours. It was then surrounded by sods of turf and logs that grew into a large fire capable of boiling the first kettle of the morning. The fire was up and running for another day and the work of the kitchen and farm could crack into action.

Straddled above the fire was the crane, which was the scaffolding from which hung the kettles, pots and ovens of the kitchen. The crane itself was a masterpiece of craftsmanship and it performed its many feats while balancing like a ballerina on one rotating leg that could swing the crane forward when required. Its long arm stretched out over the fire and two flat iron hangers dangled from it. The stronger of the two hangers was for the heavy pots and the other for the lighter pots and kettles. These hangers were skilfully controlled by a long handle that strategically levered them up and down to the required height. Down along these hangers were perforated holes and when the hanger was judged to be at the correct height an iron peg was inserted into one of these holes to hold it in position. Onto the hook at the end of this flat hanger went the pot hanger. The ends of the pot hangers curled into two iron hooks and these fitted into the ears of the pot to hang it over the fire. Mastering the skills of manipulating the hangers was the first requirement for cooking on the open fire. Pots and kettles full of boiling water required delicate balancing, otherwise the unwary cook could be flooded with disaster and two burnt or scalded legs. Bastables unwisely positioned could produce pale-faced cakes or burnt offerings. As well as being a cook, the woman of the house also required the skills of an engineer and as her cooking utensils were of heavy black cast-iron, she also required fitness, strength and dexterity. She needed to be a woman of substance and have what my father termed a good 'understanding', to keep her steady on the ground, and he was not referring to her intellectual abilities.

Her black army of cooking utensils included a large kettle for use when the whole family or a *meitheal* was gathered, and a smaller kettle when tea was required for just a few. My mother had a wide range of pots. The most impressive was the huge pot-bellied monster known as the 'pig's pot', as it was used for boiling potatoes for the pigs – potatoes that were not fit for the kitchen table came the way of the pigs. The heavy pig's pot was placed on the flag in front of the fire and the crane swung out over it so that the large pot hangers could be hooked into its ears, and then it was swung back over the fire. A hot fire licked its black bottom until the water came to the boil; when the potatoes began to disintegrate it was again swung forward and the hot water precariously drained off into a tin bucket with a jute bag over it to hold back the potatoes. This was a balancing act in time and motion to avoid a scalding waterfall. The pig's pot was often parked at the bottom of the kitchen and all food left-overs tossed into it. There was absolutely nothing wasted.

The next pot was a slightly smaller model, but still of ample capacity, and it was used to boil water on washday. Then came the potato pot, which was smaller than its big brothers but still a sizeable pot, and every day it was filled with potatoes that were boiled for the dinner, which was always at one o' clock. The healthy practice of the day was: breakfast like a king, dinner like a rich man and supper like a pauper. The potatoes that were surplus to immediate family requirements were used to feed the extended family of dogs, chickens and pigs. My grandmother's oft proclaimed creed of 'waste not, want not' was not just idle talk.

The next smaller black brother was for boiling the bacon and cabbage or turnips, which was the staple diet, all produced on the farm. We were definitely into grow your own! Once the bacon was boiled the cabbage was submerged into the same steaming pot that bubbled merrily over the fire as the potatoes eased off their jackets in the heat of the other pot beside the fire. The kitchen filled up with the smell of the approaching dinner, which flowed out over the yard and told approaching diners what was on the menu – though this was scarcely necessary as the menu seldom varied. Sauces were not considered essential to whet the appetites of the clientele and the only embellishment available was a good dollop of Coleman's mustard.

In spring the cabbage was occasionally replaced by a potful of evil-looking nettles that my mother judged to be good for our blood. Dessert was seldom on the menu, but when it was, rice, semolina or tapioca, thatched with cream from the top of the milk churn, came our way. From late summer until supplies disappeared, apples from our own trees were served stewed, boiled and roasted.

The next pot down in the assembly line was a cheeky little fellow known as the skillet, which inspired the Skillet Pot song: 'And our mother made colcannon in the little skillet pot'. He was a small, beautifully designed little lad, called into action to boil or roast a chicken or other niceties not normally on the menu. I now have one hanging off my apple tree from which the blackbirds slake their thirst and where they wash their feathers. This little skillet is probably older than myself, but unlike me is showing no signs of wear and tear. Those pots out-cooked many users.

The cook had two bastables that were used to give us our daily bread. The larger of the two was the baking container for the two big round brown cakes that my mother turned out daily to feed family and helpers. Sometimes the baking was extended to include a currant cake and, luxury of luxuries, a giant apple cake when the apple trees were groaning with apples. The smaller bastable could be used for a rare roast or to rattle up a fry of eggs and bacon, and sometimes a large, heavy frying pan was brought into action. Sometimes an empty fruit tin was used to boil eggs. The tea was left to draw in a tin teapot seated on a bed of hot coals beside the fire. All in all, the open fire was the feeder of the multitudes and the woman of the house was the wonder woman of the fireplace.

When cooking was over in the quiet of the evening she sat by the fire, took out her knitting, sewing or darning and with light from the oil lamp swinging off the wall above her head, she patched and darned and generally held the family together. She continued after the supper, which was generally around seven o'clock when the cows had been milked and the family and neighbours gathered around the fire. The open fire then became a social centre. The newspaper was read, sometimes aloud by the man of the house. The choice of paper depended on the political allegiance of the family, but usually in Cork the *Examiner*, being local, held sway. World events reported in the paper were discussed and argued over, while lessons were done by the schoolchildren, and the woman of the house maintained law and order from her chair under the lamp.

On Friday nights, with no lessons to crucify us, we children played cards – or ghost stories were often told, to our delighted horror. Later we regretted our delight in these stories as the remembered horrors threatened sleep. Before bedtime mugs of warm cocoa were dished out and sometimes toast was made on a long fork held over the glowing fire. No toast would ever taste as good as that made over a turf fire. Then the drifting off to bed began, led by the youngest. To light our way we took a sconce holding a candle. Often we read in bed and when halted by tired eyes we told each other stories, sometimes retelling the ghost stories heard earlier and frightening the life out of each other all over again.

When she had the kitchen to herself, my mother bedded down the fire for the night and arranged her laundry around it at a safe distance. Another day was done and the cricket began his lullaby behind the bellows. I loved the sound of the cricket and at that time in our schoolbook there was a poem called 'The Ant and the Cricket' and I believed that the cricket in that poem lived behind our bellows.

The Ant and the Cricket

Anonymous

A silly young cricket, accustomed to sing
Through the warm, sunny months of gay summer and spring,
Began to complain, when he found that at home
His cupboard was empty and winter was come.
Not a crumb to be found
On the snow-covered ground;
Not a flower could he see,
Not a leaf on a tree.
'Oh, what will become,' says the cricket, 'of me?'

At last by starvation and famine made bold,
All dripping with wet and all trembling with cold,
Away he set off to a miserly ant
To see if, to keep him alive, he would grant
Him shelter from rain.
A mouthful of grain
He wished only to borrow,
He'd repay it to-morrow;
If not helped, he must die of starvation and sorrow.

Says the ant to the cricket: 'I'm your servant and friend,

But we ants never borrow, we ants never lend.

Pray tell me, dear sir, did you lay nothing by

When the weather was warm?' Said the cricket: 'Not I.

My heart was so light

That I sang day and night,

For all nature looked gay.'

'You sang, sir, you say?

Go then,' said the ant, 'and sing winter away.'

Thus ending, he hastily lifted the wicket

And out of the door turned the poor little cricket.

Though this is a fable, the moral is good –

If you live without work, you must live without food.

Chapter 9

Day-old Chicks

The day-old chicks arrived by bus. Their arrival caused great excitement. They came in perforated cardboard boxes and through the holes we could see a moving mass of yellow fluff. Occasionally a little black eye peered out. A faint chorus of chirping arose from the box. Their arrival changed the face of poultry keeping on our farm.

Prior to this big step into the world of mass production all our chickens were home hatched. The procedure was simple. A huge flock of hens wandered around the yard and haggard, and at night were housed in the Jim Dillon henhouse. What, you may well ask, was a Jim Dillon henhouse? Well, after its introduction into the world of poultry, these houses became so well known that they were simply referred to as the Jim

Dillons. He happened to be the Minister for Agriculture in the late 1940s who decided that he would flood England with eggs from Ireland and to that end he had a special hen-house designed. He gave grants for their erection in farm-yards all around the country. The Jim Dillon was a simple design of a rectangular house about twelve feet long and six feet wide, with a door on the front right and two windows to the left of it. In here, arranged along the back wall, were perches on which the hens slept at night and laying boxes where they went when they felt an egg coming on. After laying, they emerged crowing with delight at their achieve-ment and letting the whole world know of their success.

My father built our Jim Dillon in the grove behind the house. We thought that it was a great step forward into the world of modern poultry keeping. Up to then the unfortu-nate hens had to be satisfied with occupying any outhouse that happened to be available around the farmyard. Their last resort, before moving into their new permanent Jim Dillon, was a loft over one of the cow stalls, which on their depar-ture we children then took over and turned into a home-made theatre. We removed their perches, erected a curtain along one end and provided a row of cow stools borrowed from the stalls below to seat the expected audience.

Around the farmyard there was a constant demand for housing for cows, pigs, calves, geese, hens and us, though our playing needs came way down the list of priorities. So, like the hens, we made use of any available space. In the summer the supply was endless as most of the animals were out in the fields, but in winter there was a bit of a struggle for occupancy. We sometimes finished up between the blocks of hay in the barn. In summer the hens, like ourselves, had the run of the whole place. They roamed freely all over the place, accompanied by an arrogant cockerel who strutted his stuff around the yard and was not above launching an attack on an unwary child. But he had a privileged position as he was the only egg fertiliser in the yard and every spring his harem provided dozens of chickens.

My mother was an expert on chicken production and when one of her hens turned broody she was promptly rounded up and provided with a soft nest of hay in either an old orange crate or timber lemonade-bottle box procured from the local shop. In this box the fluffed-out hen, like a queen on her throne, sat on her nest of eggs for about three weeks until the eggs began to crack and the little chicks peeped out at freedom. But some eggs were much ado about nothing and this was discovered by holding each one up against a crack of light at the door of a darkened room which revealed if the egg had an occupant or otherwise. Eggs without chicks were called 'glougers' and soon went rancid – the biggest insult of the day was to be called a glouger or a rotten egg; it meant that not only were you useless but that you did not smell too good either. An unfortunate state of affairs!

The baby chicks that came out of the fertilised eggs were adorable and when mother hen paraded them around the farmyard they were a delightful sight. Mother hen was a wary caretaker and kept a vigilant eye over her little flock, and all her policing skills were necessary as around the yard were many predators, including our cats. An outside source of attack was the hawk, who could suddenly swoop down and snatch one of the baby chicks in its talons then disappear up into the sky. If the mother hen saw him circling in advance of his dive she alerted us with a loud cackle and we came running to her aid.

The introduction of baby chicks by another method sidelined the role of mother hen. The name of the chicken producer that took over from her and became synonymous with the production of day-old chicks for us was Whitakers. In some mysterious way beyond my comprehension they were able to provide baby chickens by the dozen. They arrived by bus. The only bus into our town arrived late at night and as the bus stop was the local pub, the chicks spent their first night in the pub. Whitakers must have notified my mother by post of the proposed date of arrival but this was not always accurate, so it meant that my father called daily to the pub on his way home from the creamery to ascertain if they had arrived.

In preparation for their arrival a contraption known as the Hoover was moved into the kitchen. This Hoover had the appearance of a mini Vatican with a dome-shaped roof sporting a central chimney – but no white or black smoke poured from this as it simply emitted the fumes from a central oil lamp that was placed inside to keep the chicks warm. The Hoover was made of tin and had no base, so we provided a floor of newspaper and later soft hay to keep the babies warm. For comfort and cleanliness, the floor had to be changed daily as this was the chicks' complete living quarters. They were fed with pinhead oatmeal and watered by means of filling a jam pot with water, placing a saucer on top of it and then turning the whole ensemble upside down – you had to do this pretty quickly and with a certain coordination or you could be drenched in a sudden waterfall. It was a knack that you mastered with practice. The chicks drank the water that slowly ebbed out of the jam pot into the saucer. From the Hoover came a constant soft chirping sound that raised to a higher crescendo before feeding time. The chicks remained in there until they were big enough to survive in an outhouse without heat. But by then the lovely yellow downy feathers that had made them so appealing were gone and they were leggy birds, which my mother called pullets, sprouting stronger feathers. The day-old chicks had grown up.

The Little Red Hen
PJ McCall

Once a Rat and Cat and Red Hen grew fat
In the hollow oak of a glossy glen:
'Let us have a feast fit for an Eastern king,
The like of which never was seen by men!
Let us haste and make
A dark speckled cake
With plums from the land of the Saracen!'
'Let us!' says Rat. 'Let us!' says Cat.
'Let us make the cake!' says Little Red Hen.

'Who will go to the mill by the mountain rill
That tumbles o'er rocks to our grassy glen,
And get wheat ground as the wheel goes round,
Then sifted and sacked by the miller's men;
That we three may make
Our dark speckled cake
With plums from the land of the Saracen?'
'I won't!' says Rat. 'I won't!' says Cat.
'I'll do it myself!' says Little Red Hen.

'Who will elbows bare and will apron wear,

And mix the dough with housewife's ken?

Who will round the cake and set it to bake,

And watch that it may not blacken or bren?

Who will undertake

To bespeck this cake

With plums from the land of Saracen?'

'I won't!' says Rat. 'I won't!' says Cat.

'I'll do it myself!' says Little Red Hen.

'Who will take high seat with neckerchief neat,

White coiffed like the wives of great gentlemen?

Who will bend a face at saying grace,

And at end of the blessing will say Amen?

Who will eat the cake

That myself will bake

With plums from the land of the Saracen?'

'I will!' says Rat. 'I will!' says Cat.

'I'll eat it myself!' says Little Red Hen.

Chapter 10

The Light of
Other Days

Before electricity flooded our homes, revealing cob-
webs and extending our working hours, we endeavoured to light up the darkness and extend the light of day
in many ways. The windows themselves were quite small
because of the need to keep heat in and cold out, and in
farmhouses they were not framed with curtains for two reasons: the first was the cost factor, and the second the practical
reason of needing to let in as much light as possible. There
could be no deterrent to the flow of natural daylight. There
were, however, shutters but these were seldom used at night
as privacy was not high up on our list of priorities. After all,

the neighbours lived across the fields and the animals were not greatly interested in our goings on. So anyone passing the kitchen window looked in and had a preview of the interior activities before venturing inside.

As soon as dusk gathered in around the kitchen, the oil lamp was lit – but not too early, as there was always a need to spare the oil. Our childhood was all about sparing, and economical household practices. We were reared to the background anthem of: spare the matches, spare the candles, spare the oil and, the most-repeated anthem of all, spare the battery. The battery was, of course, the source of power for the much-appreciated radio in our midst. If my father had no battery to hear the news he let out a spiel about extravagant women, who, unlike his mother, knew nothing about thrift, and he regularly told us that there was enough thrown out in our house to rear another whole family. Of course, this gem of paternal ideology ran off the backs of his five daughters like water off a duck. We were, in actual fact, very sparing and, indeed, almost totally self-sufficient. Tea, sugar, matches, oil, candles and the radio battery were the only items we required from the outside world, as everything else came off the farm. But my father felt that the things that had to be bought required extra-careful management and we never quite seemed to come up to the mark. Money was scarce and very hard-earned, so spending it was an exercise of extreme caution. Everything was done to avoid being reduced to just the light of the fire or – the ultimate disaster – facing a silent radio. But this was an adult problem of which we children were mostly unaware and we treated everything with the free abandonment that is part of childhood.

The main oil lamp hung in the kitchen. Each morning the glass bowl containing the oil was lifted out of its cast-iron cradle that was attached to an arm that hinged off the wall beside the fire. This arm could be rotated sideways so that the lamp might be angled to the area beneath it requiring most light. The oil bowl of the lamp was tin, glass or brass and on top of it sat the burner for the wicks that went down into the bowl to absorb the oil. These wicks were flat, about an inch wide and made of hemp, and they came up through two matching slits in the burner; they were controlled from the side by a tiny wheel with serrated edges by which you could raise or lower the flame. Beside this wick turner was a little ladle-shaped tool known as the quencher. The flame was put out by pressing this quencher down and you raised it before lighting up at night. You could have a single burner or double burner. Fitted over the burner and held in place by a circular ring of little brass pods was the glass globe. Before the bowl was lifted out of its cradle, the globe was carefully removed to await polishing while the burner was unscrewed and laid sideways, with the wicks still in the oil. Then, by means of a funnel, additional oil was carefully poured into the bowl and the burner screwed carefully back on. The wick was then trimmed to remove the burnt edgings of the previous night and the bowl replaced in its cradle.

Next up for inspection was the delicate globe that required careful handling to avoid a crack which would be a disaster. If the globe was blackened by the previous night's smoke, as the result of inefficient lighting or quenching, it was dipped carefully into a dish of warm water and gently massaged clean with a soft cloth. Then it stood on the table to allow the surplus water to drain off and when that was achieved to the satisfaction of the woman of the house, it was gently rubbed dry and then polished to a high shine with an old vest or discarded knickers. If its state of cleanliness did not necessitate this washing, it was simply polished clean with a crumpled-up newspaper, sometimes dampened with paraffin oil. When all was to the satisfaction of the lamp cleaner, the globe was replaced and all was in readiness for the arrival of the dark.

Come twilight, the lamp lighter carefully removed the globe, turned back the quenchers and turned up the wick by means of the strategically placed wick controller. Then, when it was deemed that the wicks had absorbed the required amount of oil, a match was cracked and the wicks lit. When the flame had established itself, the wicks were lowered before replacing the globe. A too-high flame could cause the globe to crack, and this was to be avoided at all costs as globes were expensive, and as they were fragile it was difficult to bring them home safely from the nearby town. It was deemed a help to prevent the globe from cracking if a hairpin was slipped over the top edge of the globe and allowed to hang down its sides.

This was the inadequate and mellow light by which we learnt our lessons, my mother did her sewing and darning and my father read the paper. Beneath it too, cards were played and ghost stories told – and because the light did not reach into the far corners of the room it created mysterious shadows that lurked in the peripheries. This atmosphere fanned fertile imaginations which later led to checking under beds and behind doors for lurking 'pookies', or ghosts.

The other kitchen lamp was the Sacred Heart lamp, which was the tiny tot of the oil lamps and remained lighting day and night, casting a diffused red glow around the kitchen. We were always glad of this glow when as teenagers we came home late at night from the pictures or dances.

The kitchen lamp was quite basic in design, but the parlour lamp was a far grander affair. Its ridged brass leg rose elegantly out of a black ebony base that held it firmly in the centre of the sideboard. The brass leg spread up into a deep bowl which could be a rich red, regal green or brass. Some bowls were plain, but others were beautifully engraved with roses or other intricate designs, and the burner and all its attachments were brass. The globe was no different to the one in the kitchen lamp, but the shade that rested around it on an outer brass rim was the jewel in the crown. Its upper edge might be fluted and its colour match the base, but if the base was brass the shade could often be a wonderful combination of delicate colours. Because it had to emit light, the colouring was usually soft and muted, but sometimes it could be a rich red which gave off a warm glow, or a deep green which brought the world outside inside. The parlour lamp was the Grande Dame of the lamps, and she never dented her dignity by making an appearance anywhere but in the parlour.

For the bedroom, the candle and sconce was the beacon of light – though maybe not so much a beacon as a yellow flickering flame. Amazingly, children were entrusted with these to accompany them upstairs to bed and more amazingly still, there was never a resulting fire in our house. Care was instilled in us from an early age and we balanced our sconces carefully as we ascended the narrow stairs, and having arrived in the bedroom we placed them carefully on the dressing table. But not always! I have memories of pouring hot candle grease on top of the iron bedpost, plonking the candle into it and holding it firmly in position until the candle grease hardened and the candle was secure. This enabled me to read in bed, but also caused a waterfall of candle grease to drip down the bedpost and onto the floor. Every bedroom floor in the house was spattered with candle grease and one of the Saturday jobs was to go down on our knees with a blunt knife to scrape it off.

Lighting up the world outside was a different job altogether and here the storm lantern came into play. This was
also fired by oil at the base, but the wick was enclosed by a
high, all-encompassing tough globe encased in iron bars that
wound up into a long handle that enabled it to be carried
easily by hand. The globe could not be removed but could
be eased up to expose the wick for lighting. A thick globe
guarded the flame from rain and wind, and so it could be
taken out in all kinds of weather. It was used for checking
farm animals at night; and if an unexpected foray outside was
necessary in darkness, this was the accompanying light.

The flash lamp was another friend of the night traveller, be
he either walking or on a bicycle. Here too the battery had
to be saved and its little bulb replaced if it got blown.

In later years the oil lamp was replaced by the Tilly, which
gave out a much stronger light. The Tilly was also dependent
on oil, but instead of a wick it was lit by a mantle, which was
a kind of mesh that soaked up oil. An enamel or tin base held
the oil at the bottom of the lamp and a narrow pipe led it up
to the white mantle. Half-way up the pipe was a little well
and into this was poured methylated spirits, which was then
lit and the flames licked the base of the mantle. When the
mantle was judged to be sufficiently warm, you very slowly
gave a gentle push to the pump on the base. This drove oil
up into the mantle, which then ignited and burst into a blue
flame that slowly, after further gentle pumping of the oil,

turned white and gave out a good strong light. The lighting of this lamp, if not properly done, could result in a black mantle and a snorting smoking monster, but when all went well the light was a great improvement on the oil lamp.

But, of course, there were brighter days ahead and when the ESB came, all these lamps faded into oblivion and we basked in the bright electric light that lit up all our lives.

Chapter 11

Grandmother's Dresser

My grandmother's dresser was huge and occasionally she 'did it down'. That was the expression she used for the big job of emptying out this enormous piece of furniture, removing the white oil cloth, scrubbing the insides, washing the contents and putting it all back together again. Exactly as it had been!

I loved my grandmother's dresser. To me it was a book full of stories. She would recall the history of every item as it was removed. An austere, strict disciplinarian, of whom I was slightly in awe, she became a different person while she master-minded the emptying out and washing of her dresser.

Then she became a storyteller, a recaller of family history. Some things in that dresser had been in the house when she came to live there, or she had brought them with her as part of her 'bottom drawer', and some she had acquired over the years.

On the top shelf were four enormous dishes, two brown and two blue. The brown ones had been in the house before her and the blue ones she brought with her, a gift from her mother on her marriage. The brown ones had a thick base and were older than the blue ones, and my grandmother treasured them as they had been used by generations of her husband's people. These dishes were held in place by a solid rail of wood a few inches from the back of the dresser and they were taken out and used only for big occasions such as the Stations, to hold the Christmas goose, and for threshings and special family occasions, in which she was a great believer. It always amazed me how my grandmother, whom I felt was a very uncompromising woman, had settled in so amicably into our grandfather's family home and was held in the highest esteem by all her in-laws, whom she entertained regularly and regaled with their ancestral history, which she had absorbed over the years. The family photographs that had been in the house when she arrived were still there when I was a child, and at night, before going to sleep, she would tell me the stories of the pictures hanging on the bedroom wall. She was the family archivist. Widowed at an early age, she ran the farm with superb efficiency and unflinching determination, and was a better farmer than many of her male neighbours. Forthright and direct, she did not tolerate idleness in any form and regularly told me that there was nothing got from idleness only dirt and long nails. She was a good neighbour and once when challenged about being over-helpful to one of her neighbours, she retorted sharply, 'Sure, of course we must help! His mother is dead and his father is a fool.' Diplomacy was not one of her virtues.

In front of the blue and brown dishes on the dresser – and seldom used – were glasses and bowls, one containing the cartridges for my uncle's shot-gun. The sight of these cartridges glinting red and dangerous in the glass bowl filled me with disquiet. I imagined that they could take aim without the gun! One cut-glass jar had been repaired with wire, which to me was a mini miracle – this was in the era before glue and the magic that sticks everything to everything. My grandmother would look at the repaired bowl and smile meditatively: 'Oh the day that Jack broke that bowl,' she would say, 'there was "who began it". But when your great-aunt Bridget came to stay, she had magic fingers and made it as good as new.' Fixing glass with wire was unimaginable to me. When I asked tentatively why it had not just been thrown out, she gave me a scornful look: 'Child, you must master the art of making do.'

On the second shelf, also kept in place by a firm wooden

rail, were rows of dinner plates not in everyday use. These were for special occasions and years later I discovered that they were, in fact, Wedgewood, and very precious. She never filled me in on where they came from, but maybe my grandfather, who was a cattle dealer and travelled to England in pursuit of his trade, may have indulged himself after a good sale and decided to splurge on a treat for his industrious wife. In front of these plates were basins of varying sizes – a few chipped and battered, but still in use. Here too was her collection of teapots and jugs, amongst them a jam-jug which could hold three pounds of jam. The 'lustre jugs' glowed a rich golden copper brown and the china ones displayed an amazing variety of delicate rose designs. To this day I love jugs and teapots, and I think this is due to the influence of my grandmother's dresser. Some of these jugs were minus their handle, or a teapot might have a cracked cover, and she would recall the story of the mishap that had caused the damage. She might then add a story about the culprit, often a child, and would tell of the life path on which they later embarked. In this way she introduced us to some of our long-departed extended family. These maimed jugs and teapots had also become the family filing cabinet, holding bills, wartime ration books, the creamery book and old family photographs.

Part of the 'doing down' of the dresser was the removal and examination of these documents. Some judged not to be for childish viewing were quickly refolded and disappeared into her apron pocket to be later replaced where she would be able to put her hand on them when necessary. The old photographs would bring memories flooding back and stories were told about people in faraway places who had long ago been children of the house. Sometimes, if the memories were almost obscured by the mists of time, she would sit in her rocking chair and gently rock the memories back up to the surface of her mind – she would slowly nod her head in satisfaction as the story gradually eased up from the depths of her memory. After the telling, she might take the corner of her long black apron and wipe a tear from her eye. This was a side of my grandmother that was seldom seen. Then she would straighten up and briskly get on with the job on hand.

On the third shelf down came the smaller plates and cups and saucers. These were for everyday use, but some were made of china and kept for special occasions. Also in there was her own favourite china cup and saucer, which she summoned into action when she was feeling fragile and felt that the world was too much for her. Then she sometimes took to her bed and recited long rosaries to calm her spirit, and when she felt able, she rose again and carried on with life.

Beneath the shelves came the lap of the dresser, the landing place for an endless variety of objects, which could include the daily paper, usually the *Irish Press* in her case as she was a staunch republican. Accompanying it could be back numbers of *The Messenger* and *The Far East*, the flash lamp, sconces with candles – anything that people put down until they found a better place for it, but never did. Under the lap of the dresser were two large drawers, one for cutlery and the other, which may have been originally intended for tablecloths, somehow became the receptacle for valuable tools too precious to be put into the box of hammers, nails and general leftovers after odd jobs. In this drawer you could find the spirit level, an invaluable tool for judging the balance of shelves – and which my uncle once put on top of my head to judge if I was level! Then the set-square for judging angles, the rasp for shoeing horses and the awkward auger for laboriously drilling holes. These were expensive tools and not every household had them, so they were loaned around to neighbours who returned the favour with some tools not in my grandmother's drawer. The cutlery drawer had a miscellaneous collection of bone-handled knives and forks that had to be cleaned weekly. Along the front of the shelves were brass hooks off which dangled an array of little jugs. Some of these were cream jugs that were in constant use, especially during the winter months as butter was made at that time on the farm, and so there was a plentiful supply of cream, but even when it was not butter-making season, the top of the churn was skimmed for jugs of cream. Under the drawers was an open storage area for the pots and pans of the kitchen and in earlier years this had also been the hatching area for the hens and geese who were part of the farm economy.

The dresser was a large piece of furniture that stretched along half the back wall of the kitchen. Hanging off a hook at one side was my uncle's shaving strap, on which he sharpened his razor, and on the other side the family rosary beads. Sometimes here too hung a hare, rabbit or pheasant on their way to the cooking pot.

On top were stored wooden boxes containing household reserves of tea, sugar and candles. Living far from the town, which was accessible only by foot, bicycle or horse, it was necessary to be able to survive for long periods if the winter turned bad and you were snowed in for weeks, which was not unknown in the hilly region on the Cork-Kerry border. Behind these boxes, lying unobtrusively out of sight, was my uncle's shotgun, which was part of farming life. Also up there beside it, over-wintering for safety reasons, could be the lethal hay knife.

Slipped in between the timber boxes was a deep cardboard box wrapped in brown paper containing the good tablecloths, while the everyday cloth rested on the lap of the dresser. This everyday cloth was known as the 'bageen' cloth as it was made from old flour bags, and it was very functional – having covered the table for the dinner it was the receptacle for potato peelings and scraps of meat that were then gathered up and deposited in the yard for the waiting dogs. The table was a wooden one, which, with its accompanying *súgán* chairs, had to be scrubbed white weekly, so the bageen cloth kept it looking good in between.

In many ways, my grandmother's dresser was a built-in kitchen which contained everything she needed to keep both her culinary department and her farm functioning to her satisfaction.

Buried deep in the recesses of my mind, the memory of my grandmother's ritual of the dresser lay hidden and I had always hankered after one. In our old farm kitchen when I was growing up, we did not have a dresser, but had what we called a 'glass case', which, in one way, was the same, but it had glass doors at the front. This, needless to mention, was a far more practical option as it kept the utensils inside clean and dust-free. Still, to me it lacked the attraction of the open dresser that graced my grandmother's kitchen. I loved the nudity of the rows of blue and brown dishes at the top of the dresser and the rows of plates of varying sizes on the shelves down along. Interspersed with bowls, basins and jugs of a multiplicity of designs, these shelves made intriguing viewing. Without being fronted by glass doors, all of these items were in some way more accessible and told their story without a barrier between me and them. I was able to reach out to touch and smell these wonders and it enabled them to tell their true story without restraint. To me this was akin to getting into the sinews of the house and the fabric of the living therein. On my grandmother's dresser was the story of our family.

I dreamt that one day I too would own a dresser. So when we gave our jaded kitchen an overhaul in the early nineties I seized the opportunity to fulfil my dream. For years our kitchen had been the demented hub of a busy guest house and the cradle of bawling babies and rampaging teenagers – and then with the advent of a change of business and the emergence of young adults, all became civilised. This was my chance: I planned a dresser. The wish of a lifetime was about to be mine. In the end I ended up with two dressers, as an Aga holds centre stage in my kitchen so a dresser took up position at each side of it. They were made to fit the space by a friend who had the patience of Job and the expertise of Joseph, so I had the chance to recreate my grandmother's dresser. My practical friends warned that I was crazy, that it would be dusty, a home for spiders and all kinds of wildlife, and high maintenance. In other words, a health hazard. But I turned a deaf ear. After all, who can reason with a woman carrying a childhood dream?

My dresser is now with me for twenty years and yesterday I 'did it down'. Hence the writing of this chapter. Admittedly, over the years the dresser may have been a bit high-maintenance, but it more than compensated with its glow of memories spread across the entire kitchen wall. It's like a giant oil painting, telling the story of a family tree. Across the top are three large dishes that I call 'Pat Mac's dishes' – Pat is long gone and these huge dishes came out of his Mom's trunk that she brought back from America, and when Pat died he left them to my sister and her husband. When I opened a guest house in the early sixties they came my way. They were used for many years to hold shoals of slippery salmon caught in the river Bandon, which were later gutted and cooked for hungry guests. These dishes are now surplus to requirements. Too big for the dresser, they stand along the top, and with them is a large green enamel jug with a red rose that was part of my mother's bedroom set before en suite became part of Irish life. When this jug got too old for service, my mother used it to hold her baking milk, and when it began to leak, she used it for eggs. One day she asked me what would I like to have from the home place and I told her the jug; she smiled in surprise and said, 'But that old jug is leaking.' But to me that did not matter because the jug was the story of home. Beside this stands a black crucifix belonging to Uncle Jacky, my husband Gabriel's uncle, whom I considered to be a saint, and next come the large dishes from Aunty Peg's and Aunty Mary's dinner services. Then a vibrant rose-patterned platter that my sister Ellen brought from Canada, an earthenware jug that a practical sister gave me as a wedding present, and a large stock jug bought in Bandon pottery when I was feeding the masses.

As I wash these large items I think fondly of their wonderful owners, while the dishwasher cleans all the lesser plates, cups and dishes that line the shelves beneath them – with a dishwasher, a dresser is now not such a challenge. Some of these pieces were inherited from Aunty Peg, my husband's aunt, who cared for them and used them all her life, and now I do the same and they give me great joy. What really clothes family heirlooms in value are the memories they absorb over the years. Hanging off the hooks along the front of the shelves is an array of Aunty Peg's rose-patterned little cream jugs, and a white one with a gold band that was given to me in 1989 as a gift by Mary Cronin of Tig Nonie of Boherbue, where we filmed the programme 'I Live Here' that I made with RTÉ after my first book, *To School through the Fields*, was published. A little china toast rack belonging to Mrs C, who came to stay with us for a few days after her husband died and stayed until she died fourteen years later. This elegant little toast rack tells her story – she came out of one of the great houses of Ireland, and downstairs into our corner house she brought the whiff of 'upstairs'. Sitting beside this is a crazy-patterned jumping cow that a young friend brought back from his first foray abroad. This cow has absolutely nothing to do with heirlooms and has jumped straight out of today's world, but the thoughtfulness of the giver was heart-warming. An ancient salt, pepper and

mustard dish belonging to my mother sits beside it and then comes Aunty Peg's much-treasured milk jug, often used now to hold flowers from my garden. I am a great believer in constantly using all the old family bits and pieces. No point in letting them gather dust on the shelf to be taken out for my wake!

My grandmother's dresser left me with many memories, as I am sure so did the dressers of many grandmothers. Maybe you remember your own grandmother's dresser?

The Old Woman of the Roads

Padraic Colum

O, to have a little house!
To own the hearth and stool and all!
The heaped up sods against the fire,
The pile of turf against the wall!

To have a clock with weights and chains
And pendulum swinging up and down!
A dresser filled with shining delph,
Speckled and white and blue and brown!

I could be busy all the day
Clearing and sweeping hearth and floor,
And fixing on their shelf again
My white and blue and speckled store!

I could be quiet there at night
Beside the fire and by myself,
Sure of a bed and loth to leave
The ticking clock and the shining delph!

Och! but I'm weary of mist and dark,
And roads where there's never a house nor bush,
And tired I am of bog and road,
And the crying wind and the lonesome hush!

And I am praying to God on high,
And I am praying Him night and day,
For a little house – a house of my own
Out of the wind's and the rain's way.

Chapter 12

Dancing on Blankets

In today's world of cascading hot showers and an endless supply of hot water on demand, with washing machines effortlessly rendering our clothes whiter than white and tumble dryers tossing underwear bone-dry at our feet, there is very little credit due to any of us for being cleaner than clean and smelling like roses. But it took Herculean effort from the women of past generations to keep their families looking good, not to mention smelling good, particularly in the farming world where the boundary line between the farmyard and the home was often not easily discernible. As the animals were the bread-and-butter of the family, and high on the priority care list, they sometimes had to be brought across that line. So it was not unknown for the hens

and chickens to visit the kitchen and for the mother pig to be brought in to have her *bonhams* in the kitchen or back kitchen, and baby lambs and piglets to start their life in a box by the open fire – unimaginable in today's world of hygiene and health-and-safety, but then all part of keeping the wolf from the door. The result of all this proximity to the animal world resulted in a constant struggle to keep family, clothes and house clean; in every house in the country it was an ongoing battle to keep back the tide of dirt and grime.

Open fires too coughed out smoke and ash dust, and as there were no hoovers or electric floor cleaners, this meant going down on your knees to scrub and polish. When the wooden floors and stairs were scrubbed clean with a tough bristle brush, known simply as the 'scrubbing brush', they were then polished with a lump of beeswax or Mansion's floor polish, and afterwards glossed up with a mop or redundant knickers or long johns.

Keeping the house clean was a big job, but keeping the clothes and bodies likewise was an undertaking of gigantic proportions. The main tool for this operation was the wash tub, but the tin bath was also used. The wash tub was made of heavy oak slats held together by iron bands and had two raised, perforated ears by which it could be lifted and carried around. This was a job for the fit and well. Its working companion was the wash-board, a solid flat piece of wood with a tin ridged face against which the clothes were scrubbed vigorously to evict the grime. Prior to the arrival of the wash-board, the 'dolly' had done the job – this was a brass or copper moon-shaped drum with a perforated base and a long handle, and the washer woman grasped the handle and thumped it up and down on the offending garments. The wash-board was probably viewed as a big improvement in its day. The Monday wash was carried out weekly in all Irish farm kitchens.

Early on Monday mornings the wash-tub action began with the washer woman – usually the woman of the house – donning her cross-overalls and making herself further water resistant with an apron tied across her front. Straight after breakfast, the large, iron, three-legged wash pot was hoisted by two people onto the hangers over the fire and skilfully adjusted into position so that a big fire could fit beneath it, and yet it would not be too high as it had to receive buckets of water drawn from the spout at the end of the yard or from the barrels full of rainwater at the gable end. It took a blazing fire underneath the pot to bring the cold water to the boil, and then this scalding water was ladled out by means of a small tin bucket to the waiting wash tub, that rested on the back of a súgán chair secured in position by the leg of the kitchen table. When the tub was sufficiently full with boiling water, the temperature was rendered bearable by additional buckets of cold water drawn from the spout. The wash-board was placed in position and the carbolic soap, which came in white and red, applied to the clothes – and the Monday wash began. The first washing powders to appear in the shops were Rinso and Lux, and they replaced the bars of soap.

First into the tub were the sheets and pillow cases, and as the material in most of these was linen, twill or good-quality cotton, they were no lightweights. After a good soaking in the warm water they were pulled up over the wash-board, lathered with soap, and then scrubbed up and down against the ridged board. Then they were squeezed and laid aside on the table. Then came the ample Horrock's workshirts that were far-reaching enough to cover all vital statistics in cold weather. Next in was the underwear, and those were the days before nylon or drip-dry, so these were all made of natural fibres and, though very comfortable for the wearer, they were not kind to the washer. But the real villains of the piece were the clothes worn for the work on the farm especially the overalls made of a very heavy twill. All these working clothes were made from tough, serviceable materials and were a nightmare to get clean – and some were lathered with mud and cow dung, so the washing brought plenty of sweat to the brow of the washer woman. As the washing proceeded, the water in the tub was changed regularly and when all items were washed, the rinsing began.

Then some of the whites were put into the pot over the fire to be boiled. This removed any tough stains left in them and brought them up to a brilliant white. The removal of these

steaming whites from the boiling pot was a hazardous undertaking, usually done with the handle of a brush that required
the finely honed skills of an expert juggler. All this activity
was moist and messy, and slowly the kitchen filled with steam
and the floor took on the appearance of a mini lake. While all
this was going on, the fire required constant attention to keep
up the hot-water supply. Slowly the dry pile of dirty clothes
dwindled and the washed and rinsed pile grew higher on the
kitchen table, from where they were bucketed to the clothes
line at the end of the yard. Here they were pinned in place
by wooden clothes pegs bought from travelling gypsies. Some
delicate whites were soaked in Reckitt's Blue to make them
whiter than white. Heavy wool jumpers, mostly home-knit,
got special treatment to avoid shrinkage.

Of course, getting this mountain of washing dry was
totally dependent on the weather, which, with our Irish cli-
mate, could be a real hit-and-miss affair. Garments that did
not fit on the clothes line were laid over hedges and bushes,
which worked well in good weather but not so well when
a wet bush and garment developed a clinging relationship.
Sometimes sheets and whites were laid out on the clean grass
of the fields as my mother believed that this rendered them
cleaner, brighter and more sweet-smelling – though the ash
tree had to be avoided at all costs as it could drip down a
permanent stain. In fine weather all was good. After a warm
sunny day, bringing in armfuls of sweet-smelling, dry wash-

ing in the evening was a lovely experience. It smelt of wild woodbine, sunshine and the world outside. I recall it today every time I see washing flying high on a clothes line. Later in the week some of these clothes returned to the kitchen where late at night my mother hung them on the backs of chairs around the fire to air them. It was nice then to put your head in between the dry sheets and sniff their fresh outdoor smell.

Come Saturday, the ironing of Sunday dresses and shirts began. The interior of the iron was removed from the outer cover and thrust into the belly of the fire, where it remained until it was red hot, and then was carefully eased in through the back door of the outer cover of the iron again. The kitchen table was covered with a blanket, then a sheet, and it became the ironing board. All this could be a hazardous undertaking, requiring care and caution to avoid scorching the woman in charge of the iron or a burnt patch adorning the breast of a best blouse.

The greatest praise that my mother could ever pay to a day was to say that it was a great day for washing blankets. It was not the actual washing to which she was referring, of course, but the drying, because drying wool blankets required a dry, windy day that would blow the blankets high into the air and dry out their dense wool fibre. So you never undertook the yearly job of washing blankets unless the weather was dry, windy and settled, with a good weather forecast to back it up. Not an easily attainable blend. But if wet sheets were undesirable around the house, wet blankets were a no-no; this is probably where the expression 'a wet blanket' got its origins – not great company in any shape or form!

The actual washing of the heavy wool blankets was a weighty procedure whereby the wash tub, filled with a blanket and fluffed up with warm, soapy water, was placed on the floor or out in the yard, and the women and children stepped in and danced on top of the blanket acting as agitators to extract the dirt! Children, of course, loved this and had great fun washing the blankets. Then the dripping blanket had to be lifted out by two able-bodied women and given a slight squeeze while the water was changed for rinsing, and then there was more dancing. After that, the real marathon of squeezing as much water as possible out of the sodden blanket began. This was not a job for the faint-hearted – of body or mind. The two squeezers stood at either end of the blanket and they squeezed in opposite directions while a waterfall cascaded down. This squeezing continued until the waterfall turned into a stream, then a trickle, then a drip, until finally there was nothing left to extract. The blanket then got a firm shake and was taken to a strong clothes line, which at the time was made of wire known as 'creamery wire', which was strung between two trees. Or the blanket might be laid across an accommodating bush or hedge. It was brought in at night to avoid absorbing the night dew, but it took a few days before the blanket, fluffy and smelling of fresh air and wild flowers, could be folded away in the blanket press.

The blankets would make a welcome reappearance when chilly winter crept in the bedroom windows. In the years before we insulated out the cold and heated our homes, warm wool blankets were a necessity to survive the damp and cold that penetrated our roofs and whistled in through our single-glazed, loosely fitting windows. The only heating in most houses then was the open fire in the kitchen, or the occasionally lit parlour fire, and on rare occasions a fire in the bedroom – but much of the heat disappeared up the chimney or through the windows or out under the doors. Warm clothes – and especially blankets – were the answer to the problem.

Some tablecloths, special runners for mantelpieces, the collars of men's shirts and special dresses were starched, which was a tortuous exercise. The starch that came with a cheery Red Robin on the side of the box was anything but a cheery undertaking. It had to be blended with boiling water until at a certain point it 'turned', it then became a swirling grey mess into which the article was dipped and then whipped out and, after a slight squeeze, allowed to drip-dry. If you had got the mixture right, the cloth or garment achieved the desired level of rigidity as it dried. But if you got your mixture wrong, the collar could turn into a cut-throat razor and the tablecloth into a rigid sheet capable of skinning the knees of your diners. It required experience to master the art of starching. And if not carried out expertly, ironing a starched item could be a sticky affair, with the iron and garment refusing to part company.

Keeping clothes clean was a big job, but keeping the wearer likewise was also a challenge. This revolved around the wash tub or a tin bath. The water had to be boiled as for washing the clothes, but instead of these going into the bath or tub it was the wearer who went in. Children were rotated on Saturday nights in front of the kitchen fire, but adults had to retire to their chilly bedrooms to do the necessary to the best of their ability with limited facilities and a still more limited supply of hot water. The bedroom set for this was a wide pan and tall jug, often with a matching soap tray and chamber pot. The water was brought up from downstairs in the jug and there was an accompanying bucket for the used water. Decorative earthenware sets were used mostly for special visitors and are now found in antique shops. For everyday use the tone was lowered to enamel.

So when we step merrily into our power-showers, recline in our jacuzzis, or without a second thought toss our laundry into our automatic washing machine, let's be grateful for the times in which we live and salute our grandmothers, who, despite all odds, still succeeded in keeping a clean face and stepping out in style.

The Table and the Chair

Edward Lear

Said the Table to the Chair,

'You can hardly be aware,

'How I suffer from the heat,

'And from chilblains on my feet!

'If we took a little walk,

We might have a little talk!

'Pray let us take the air!'

Said the Table to the Chair.

II

Said the Chair unto the Table,

'Now you know we are not able!

'How foolishly you talk,

'When you know we cannot walk!'

Said the Table, with a sigh,

'It can do no harm to try,

'I've as many legs as you,

Why can't we walk on two?'

III

So they both went slowly down,
And walked about the town
With a cheerful bumpy sound,
As they toddled round and round.
And everybody cried,
As they hastened to their side,
'See! the Table and the Chair
'Have come out to take the air!'

IV

But in going down an alley,
To a castle in a valley,
They completely lost their way,
And wandered all the day,
Till, to see them safely back,
They paid a Ducky-quack,
And a Beetle, and a Mouse,
Who took them to their house.

V

Then they whispered to each other,
'O delightful little brother!
'What a lovely walk we've taken!
'Let us dine on Beans and Bacon!'

So the Ducky, and the leetle
Browny-Mousy and the Beetle
Dined, and danced upon their heads
Till they toddled to their beds.

Chapter 13

Tea in the Parlour

The parlour was the formal room of the house and was the room where the family photographs were displayed on the walls, mantelpiece and sideboard. Our ancestors regarded the ritual of having family photographs taken as serious business. They had a great sense of family history and even though money was not plentiful in many families, they still stretched the budget to cover the expense of formal family portraits. It was in the parlour that these serious-faced family members were on show, often enshrined in gilt-edged frames. In our parlour my stern-faced, bearded grandfather stood to attention, while from another wall my paternal grandmother smiled benignly across at him. For some reason they were not united in photography, but their

presence gave us a sense of who we were. Both had died before I was born.

My parents, looking unbelievably young and solemn as they faced into a strange new world in their wedding photograph, graced the wall over the long sideboard. At one end of this sideboard was the gramophone and beside it, in their brown paper sleeves, the 78 records. These records included John McCormack, Delia Murphy, Fr Sydney McEwan and Joseph Locke, as well as a collection of waltzes, jigs and reels. This gramophone had one annual holiday from the parlour when it visited the kitchen for the twelve days of Christmas. Beside the gramophone along the old oak sideboard, was the photograph of aunts and uncles who had once been the children of the house, and underneath it were two deep drawers, one for cutlery and the other for bottles. Maybe our ancestors were into bottles of whiskey and brandy, but my mother favoured sherry and port wine, though sometimes a bottle of holy water could be found among her drinks collection.

Parlour fireplaces were either black iron or marble, and ours was a mottled brown marble with a black iron inset fronted on the floor by dark brown marble tiles with a similar edging. Along the mantelpiece were tiny, quaint china and silver high-heeled shoe ornaments, and photos of American cousins impeccably dressed for First Communions, or handsome army officers one of whose parents, perhaps, had left this house many years previously.

On either side of the fireplace was a pair of upright brown leather armchairs that guaranteed no slouching and a one-armed sofa which invited elegant reclining rather than a relaxed curl-up with a book. The one window, set in the three-foot thick stone wall, had shutters that were seldom closed and this was the only window in the house adorned by curtains. These were of white lace and draped over a long wooden pole, and were more ornamental than practical as they were totally see-through. But they set the tone of the room, which was gracious. This was a room used for special occasions only, and these included the hosting of family wakes.

All our ancestors were waked in the parlour. Before it became fashionable for the coffin to be brought to the house for the wake, an iron bed with brass railings was dismantled and brought down from upstairs. It could well be that the person to be waked might have been born in that bed. It was re-assembled in the centre of the parlour and it was not unusual for people to have put aside special bed linen for this occasion. A local woman, well accustomed to the practice, laid out the dead person for the wake. People were usually laid out in a sombre brown habit or in their own clothes, with their rosary beads draped around their hands, but my mother, who had been a Child of Mary, was laid out in her lovely blue cloak. Candles were placed in brass candlesticks and arranged around the bed, and often these candlesticks made their way around the townland for all the wakes and were sometimes brought along by the woman who did the laying out. Then the neighbours gathered to say the rosary and they stayed in relays as long as the wake lasted, remaining there overnight to pray and keep the family company until it was time for the funeral. The rosary would be led at different times by a member of the family or a supportive neighbour. No priest visited the house, and the family and neighbours took care of everything; the first time a priest was involved was when the funeral arrived at the church. People sat around the parlour and chatted, and often the younger members of the family heard stories about their deceased loved one from old neighbours who had known them long before their own time.

Most of the parlour furniture was rather upright and staid, but the rocking chair compensated for the rigidity of its seating companions as it was covered in rich tapestry and was warm, inviting and comfortable. In it, you could surround yourself with soft cushions and rock gently back and forth in front of the fire. To this day I love rocking chairs and think that no other seating is as soothing to the mind and body. In the originally designed well-sprung rocking chair you can read, knit or rock a baby or yourself to sleep. They are extremely comfortable but still very supportive of bad backs, which is why President JF Kennedy had one in the Oval Office, I imagine.

The parlour came into action for big occasions such as Christmas, the stations or on the arrival of special visitors, usually returning Americans whose ancestors had left the house decades before. Then there was a flurry of activity disturbing sleeping spiders and putting a *snas* or shine on everything in sight. First, the lace curtains were whipped off and carefully washed. If it was a big overhaul, it might include distempering the walls. Our parlour walls were a dark rose colour, while my grandmother favoured a royal blue. Distemper came in powder form in a cardboard box and was diluted with water; it was applied with a special distemper brush, which was smaller than a white-washing brush and had a wider bristle than a paintbrush. As it was water-based, it had to be applied carefully to avoid spattering all around it. The timber sash window was painted with a hard gloss Uno paint, diluted with turpentine. Later, when wallpaper became available, it was widely favoured as it covered uneven wall surfaces. Varnish was applied liberally to all chair legs, table legs and the sideboard. The parlour ware was washed and the cutlery cleaned and the rug in front of the fire taken out and given a good shake. Then the floor was washed and waxed, and finally the fire was lit. With the fire lit and the parlour quiet, I loved to slip in there in the gathering dusk, sit into the rocking chair and gently rock myself back and forth, watching the fire cast shadows across the low ceiling.

On the morning of the stations the parish priest positioned himself beside this fire and cocked a listening ear to the transgressions of the townland while his curate said Mass in the kitchen. The stations were allocated by townland and how often you had them depended on how many houses were in your station area. You could have a spring or autumn station, and if the timing did not suit you, you could swap with a neighbour, though that seldom happened. After the Mass, the priest collected the station dues and when their name was called each householder stepped forward with their contribution; then he enquired who was taking the next station and everyone would know who was next in line.

For the station breakfast in our house the table was adorned with my mother's best linen tablecloth, which was washed, blued and starched to rigidity. Her fine china with matching egg cups, which had been a wedding gift from her mother, graced the table. 'Loaf sugar', which we ungraciously called 'lump sugar', was standard station fare and for this my mother had a fancy sugar tongs. The butter had been curled into decorative rolls the previous day – this was done with two wooden butter spades, dipped in warm water and a pinch of salt; there was a special art in tossing and patting the butter, or you could end up with dish full of mushy butter. Toast and boiled eggs was the standard breakfast of the day.

Afterwards, with the departure of the priests, we scoffed the left-overs, especially any sweet cake, which was one of the luxuries of the stations. Later in the day we had trifle and custard. That night more neighbours and family friends gathered and an ad-lib concert was held – and you either sang, recited or played a musical instrument as there was no such thing as a non-participant.

Chapter 14

Cow Time

To look into the eyes of a cow is a very calming experience – you are looking into two pools of tranquility. That's the reason I have a painting of a cow in the recess over the Aga in my kitchen. She looks out placidly at all the comings and goings, and breathes peace and mindfulness into the air. I first saw her in an art gallery next to the RTÉ studio in Cork. I was too early for my interview, so I went into the gallery to pass the time while waiting. Doing a live interview can be a bit unnerving, but this cow looked at me across the gallery and breathed calmness. Like St Teresa of Avila, she seemed to reassure me and say: all will be well. And so it was! I told this beautiful cow: you are coming home with me – that is, if you are not fetching the price of prime

beef. It turned out that she was affordable, so later that evening she was with me on the bus home to Innishannon. She settled very well into her new stall and is much admired by all who view her, though what people think does not put in or out on my cow. Other people's opinions do not upset or delight cows; they are immune to all of that human baggage!

My love affair with cows began at a very early age. You could say that we grew up together. As a young child I watched with horror and delight as the baby calf thrust its way into the world – horror at the moaning pains of the cow in labour, and then delight to see the tiny white hooves appear behind the water bag, and slowly the little head, until finally the whole combination of calf, afterbirth and mucus slithered onto the clean bed of straw that was waiting to receive it in the channel of the stall. The baby calf ejected a pad of tissue out of its mouth, and my father helped in the process. Then he eased it onto its wobbly feet and guided it to the manger under the mother's head, where she proceeded to lick it clean. Watching the amazing transformation that now took place always fascinated me as the cow's long, rough tongue whipped like a giant sponge across the calf, and the little creature changed from being an inert mass of bones and mucus into a shining, gorgeous little calf, its glistening coat now changed into a mass of tiny curls. Once on its feet, the calf nuzzled its way back along its mother's side until it reached her giant udder from where, in anticipation of its arrival, nourishing colostrum, which we called beast-ings, was already dripping – this contained the initial laxa-tives and protective qualities the calf needed. Mother and calf knew exactly what to do and had the calving taken place out in the field, they would have worked it out between them. However, if complications set in, they might need a mid-wife, and that was where my father came to the rescue. And because herds of cows at that time remained on farms for generations, he knew the cows who were easy 'calvers', as he termed it, and those who would have difficulty calving. The cows, of course, all had individual names and were almost part of the extended family.

The baby calves were soon separated from their mothers and put into their own house, where they were fed morning and evening with the cow's milk; then, gradually, they were weaned off that and onto what we called 'creamery milk'. This was the milk that came back from the creamery after it had been put through various processes to extract the ingre-dients to make butter, cream and cheese. The calves of dif-ferent months were segregated into separate houses, where their bedding of straw or old hay was changed daily. They romped around and were a pleasure to visit. Full of curiosity, they would stretch out their necks, inviting you to rub their soft, downy faces, and they loved to lick our outstretched fingers. In the early days of introducing them to drink out of a bucket, we would dip our fingers into the milk and let them suck it off, which helped them get accustomed to drinking without the comfort of their mothers. This was their weaning process.

Come the warm days of early summer they got their first taste of the great outdoors. When the door of their house was first opened, they stood still in confusion and had to be coaxed out into the sunlight, where they felt their way gingerly. Then we shepherded them gently into a nearby field. There they were left to their own devices.

At first they were in awe of this great unknown world. They stood transfixed by the mystery and wonder of it all. Was this possible – a world without barriers? Then one brave little fellow would step tentatively forward and, discovering nothing to stop him, take a second step. Then it dawned on him that there were no barriers and the exultation of freedom shot through him. He was free to do whatever he wanted and he gave a wild buck into the air! Whipping a triumphant tail into a circle, he raced down the field, filled with elation, and was soon followed by all the others. They were free! It was a race of sheer delight. It was such a joy to watch them savour their first taste of freedom. And when they reached the river they discovered yet another whole amazing world to be enjoyed.

They stayed out in those fields all through summer where they grew from soft baby calves into long leggy teenagers. Then, with the arrival of winter, they had to be brought back up to the farmyard to be housed away from the winter cold. And they did not like it one little bit! They had tasted freedom and did not want to give it up. Coming back into the confines of a stall after the delights of the great outdoors was not on their agenda. They protested and made many dashes for freedom as we corralled them into the confining stalls. But finally man-power overcame cow-power, and gradually they accepted the inevitable, especially when it was laced with sweet-smelling hay for supper. They grew into sturdy young yearlings and then the males were sold off, while, with the help of the bull who was part of the herd, the females became young mothers themselves.

The cows spent the summer grazing the fields and were brought in morning and evening to the stalls for milking. They were so accustomed to this ritual that once you came into the field they turned big, trusting eyes in your direction and filed obediently towards the gate. There can be no more relaxing start to a day than to walk though a dewy field behind a bawn of cows. Cows are never in a hurry and resist being rushed. A leisurely amble comes naturally to them and they gradually slow you down to their rhythm.

This was the era before milking machines when milking was done by hand, with the milker sitting on a three-legged stool beside the cow. As you sit with your head resting against the calm, warm flank of a cow, she draws you into her peaceful, unruffled world. Initially, the spray of milk would hit the bottom of the tin bucket with a rasping, metallic sound, but as the bucket gradually filled with milk this changed to a soft melodious murmur, and on entering the stall you would know from the sound what stage of milking had been reached. The full buckets of milk were then carried out to a stand where tanks or churns waited, covered with muslin to strain the impurities from the milk.

After breakfast the milk was carried to the local creamery in the pony and cart. The creamery queue was where farmers met daily for a chat and kept up with local events. The queue was an open-air social club. Here farmers discussed their milk yield, the creamery cheque and all their farming problems: it was the 'men's shed' of its day, and part of the work plan of the farm.

In summer, farming was a pleasure, but in winter it was a different story. Cows stayed in overnight, which increased the work load, as they had to be fed and their houses cleaned daily. After morning milking they went out into the fields for the day and their stalls were brushed out; over the winter high dunghills piled up outside the stall doors. Big bundles of hay were drawn with pikes to fill up the mangers at their heads, and this greeted them when they arrived back in the evening. After the evening milking they settled down and chewed the cud, then slept quietly through the night. A stall full of cows chewing the cud must be one of the most peaceful places in the world – and I wonder if we humans could

chew the cud would we have a more peaceful world? Every night before going to bed, my father lit the storm lantern and went out like Florence Nightingale to check that all was well in the bovine world. In spring the dunghills were piked into the horse and butt, and drawn out into the fields where the whole lot was spread out as fertiliser. Artificial fertiliser had yet to make its appearance – though ignorant of the term, we were organic farmers!

Chapter 15

When We Sported and Played

When we were children various jobs had to be done before we could have fun – and to me the jobs were the high jump between us and a great time. Once that fence was cleared, we were free. Now, though, I realise the wisdom of the poet Patrick Kavanagh when he spoke of wonder not coming through a chink that was too wide. I see now that the jobs sharpened our appreciation of our fun time. Once they were out of the way we headed for whatever play area was in favour at the time – the grove, the barn or the haggard.

Hide-and-go-seek was one of the favourite games and in

this the seeker put their face into their hands to block off vision and counted out loud to twenty. While the count was going on, the hiders vanished in all directions. In summer we had a wide area we could use, and we might disappear up trees, down between blocks of hay in the barn or into the horses' mangers. It could take hours to unearth us all. The barn was the greatest place to hide, as burrowing down under layers of hay rendered you totally invisible. However, if you went down too deep you could not breathe, and if you slipped down between the blocks of hay you could get trapped, so a certain amount of caution had to be exercised. But it had huge appeal because, despite the hazards, it was the best hiding place of all. The one problem, though, was the dogs, who might sniff you out and give the game away. A quick means of discovery for the seeker was to jump on top of all the hay in the barn; a reclining body, being far less supple than soft hay, was soon discovered. The unfortunate hider quickly came to the surface when the seeker jumped on a sensitive body part.

Usually during this game some Scarlet Pimpernel invariably would find a hideout in some obscure place and make themselves absolutely invisible. Then the search went on forever and this drove the rest of us mad. We would implore the hider to give up, but a strong determination not to be found arose in the hider and an equal stubbornness to succeed drove on the seeker. Eventually, after a long time, the hider might be found, or the seeker simply gave up. It was a great triumph if the seeker gave up and often the hider then took a circuitous route out of the hide so that it would be good for another time – but by then the other hiders might have changed sides and become self-appointed seekers who were on the lookout to discover the hide for themselves.

In the winter this game took place indoors and the hiding places were under beds, behind coats hanging in wardrobes or beneath clothes in presses. When the game was over, wardrobes and presses were usually less tidy, but we did serve as dust absorbers under beds and often emerged with a decidedly fluffy look!

Another favourite game was Blind Man's Buff. For this game the supposedly blind man had a towel wrapped firmly around their face, totally obliterating vision. Silence descended for a count of ten and the participants tiptoed quietly around the kitchen and took up positions in out-of-the-way corners, under the tables, behind and under chairs, or in the dark hole at the back of a deep press under the stairs – though in there I was always afraid I would meet a mouse, or worse, in the dark.

Then the blind man went around the kitchen with outstretched hands, trying to touch the silent, ducking and diving opponents. First to be caught had to be identified by means of a body feel. Once identified, they then became the blind man. Sometimes, in summer, this game was played in the barn, where there was empty space because blocks of hay had been eaten over the winter and had yet to be replaced. The barn was far more spacious than the kitchen, so it proved a greater challenge.

In summer we played Doggy Sail Away. We blocked up the *glaishe* that carried the water from the fields around the house down to the river and made a big pool where we launched our 'doggies'. These were sticks collected from under the trees in the grove. Why we called them doggies rather than boats I have no idea – maybe because dogs were more of our world than boats, and we knew that dogs could swim. Then we released the blockade and the *glaishe* carried off our crafts. As the water was going downhill it moved rapidly and carried our doggies quickly downstream. We ran along the bank, directing our doggies with long sticks, and each 'captain' hoped that their boat would win the race. Sometimes the vessel got sucked into side-streams and had to be manoeuvred back out, which meant that you lost your position in the race. The first to reach a certain point downstream was the winner. On the way home from school in summer we played Doggy Sail Away in the river, which, being a wider waterway, provided more fun, though we had to be more careful because in our exuberance we could follow the doggies into deep water.

Also on the way home from school we played Frog Jump. In this game all but one player crouched down in a long line of frogs and the challenge for the last man standing at the end was in jumping cleanly over all the frogs. Sometimes the jumper had to put their hands on a frog's shoulders to get over the 'hurdles', and sometimes this gave a mean frog an opportunity to give a sudden lurch, causing the high jumper to land on the ground. He was then disqualified. If, however, he had a clear round, the last frog took up the challenge next. A bit like the Grand National, there were a lot of mishaps and crash landings, but whereas in the Grand National there was a steward's enquiry to solve problems, we simply had long, heated arguments that could finish up with a few flattened frogs. The last upstanding frog was the winner.

On our route from school there was a high hill and in winter it was muddy and wet and turned into a skating slope. We crouched down on our haunches and using our heavy studded boots as skates we sped down the slope and upended at the bottom – we had no skis to effect an elegant halt! When snow and ice came, this was even better and we sped down the ice at a much faster rate.

Racing each other was part of every journey and we were hugely competitive. We raced each other up and down to the river bank, and back and forth to the meadows in summer. My brother and older sisters competed in the local sports – Banteer Sports were the big event – and in preparation for this they used us younger ones as rival running competitors. The result was that we were all as fit as mountain goats. Later, my brother formed a boxing club, and our barn became the boxing ring. All the local young fellows gathered there every night and the Queensberry rules were observed, guaranteeing fair play, more or less. If my brother needed to practise at odd hours and was short of a sparring partner, I was the first sub. A punch bag hung off the rafters of the barn in an effort to turn us all into Cassius Clays.

In school the boys played football in their side of the yard. Their ball was made from a collection of sodden newspapers rolled into a large ball around an old sock, tied with hay twine, and then allowed to dry. Over time, from wetting and drying, it hardened into a fairly hard lump. But better by far was the ball made from the pig's bladder. When a pig was killed the bladder was put aside to be blown up later, then seasoned up the chimney. After a few months it was almost the real thing – though the goalie was a long way from a line-up of leather balls behind the goal posts.

In the girls' side of the yard we played Cat and Mouse, which required a large number of participants. The players formed a long line with each half facing in opposite directions and at one end of the line was the cat and at the other the mouse. The aim was for the cat to catch the mouse. The whole line began to move in a clockwise direction, at first slowly, but gradually gathering speed until it worked up to a total spin, with the line of girls swinging the cat hoping to catch the line swinging the mouse. Hands were firmly gripped because a sudden break in the line could lead to bodies being littered all over the place. But the most vital hands to be held were those of the cat and the mouse. If these were released at this breakneck speed they might spin into orbit. Once when I was the mouse, my hand-holder let go and I crashed hard into the school wall. Afterwards, if I was ever proving awkward in a family argument, one of my sisters would proclaim, 'Ah sure, poor Alice, she hit her head off the school wall.'

Toys were as scarce as hen's teeth when we were children. I got a doll from Santa when I was about six and she saw me through to my teenage years. Like me, her head had a crash with a hard surface early in life – she slipped off the rocking chair onto the marble fender of the parlour fireplace and suffered brain damage. An older sister did major surgery, fitting her with a rigid bonnet that gave her the appearance of having a pain in the neck, but it held her head in place. Her name was Katie Maria, and she was the love of my life, together with two small wooden horses that I got from my godfather; I christened them Jerry and James after our two farm horses. Apart from these toys, statues provided additional playmates and there was no shortage of them in Irish homes at the time. Baby Jesus, St Theresa and St Joseph may not have been very flexible or cuddly, but they could still be used as characters in a make-believe world. Empty reels from my mother's sewing machine became the wheels for little wooden carts and, with a bit more ingenuity and a few rubber bands, also formed wobbly tractors. Stronger elastic, or the strip of a bicycle tube, carefully attached to a skilfully pared-down claw-like piece of wood, created a catapult that we fancied as a deadly weapon – but we were no Davids, so Goliath would never be slain by one of us!

At an early age we were introduced to playing cards and to the card games of Forty Five, One Hundred and Ten, Beggar My Neighbour and Donkey, all of which could cause great excitement, but also long arguments. Sometimes if things got out of hand, my mother confiscated the cards and insisted on a ceasefire, or in desperation she might announce that it was time to say the rosary. A collective groan of protest would go up, but she always turned a deaf ear.

We played Shop for hours. A makeshift shop would be erected under the trees in the grove. The shelves teetered between the branches, and the counter was an old abandoned rafter, riddled with rusty nails. An unwary customer could have a finger punctured while picking up her change. Of course, everybody wanted to be the shopkeeper and before the shop opened for business there was always a stand-up row as to who would be behind the counter – there was the strong possibility of having all shopkeepers and no customers in our shop! After all, when we went to town *we* were customers and the most envied position was the one behind the counter where you had access to sweets, ice-cream and buns,

rare treats in our world. But the merchandise in our shop in
the grove was a far cry from such luxuries and were mostly
of the abandoned variety; and there was no need to encourage our clientele to buy Irish as they had no other choice.
We sold stones, goose wings, empty jam pots and mouse
traps that had served their time and put paid to many mice.
We searched the house for empty boxes, and once when a
sophisticated neighbour came home from England she gave
us her empty powder boxes. Not only did they look gorgeous, they smelt heavenly too and we felt that our shop had
been given a great lift.

One piece of merchandise, however, nearly gave my father
a heart attack. He had purchased strychnine to evict the rats
that were attacking his grain loft and he hid the bottle high
up in the rafters of the turf house, where he deemed it to be
safely out of reach. The very next day we opened the door of
the turf house and this lovely blue bottle glinted in the light
and caught our attention. A ladder was brought into action
and the bottle taken down and carried to the shop, where
it took pride of place on our shelf. Every evening our old
neighbour, Bill, would call to our shop and he made life very
exciting as he bargained and argued with us about prices
and goods. He made us feel like a real shop. That evening,
however, he spotted the bottle and without a word of debate
offered a substantial amount, then quickly disappeared with
his purchase. We were a bit taken aback at the sudden loss of

our lovely blue bottle – not half as taken aback, though, as my father when Bill arrived into the kitchen with the bottle of strychnine. We could have had a customer wipe-out! But our currency was environmentally friendly, consisting of dried-out crab apples, haws and sloes, the pounds, shillings and pence in our shop. If the weather was unkind, the shop slid to the ground and had to be rebuilt the following day in a new location. We were the first of the Pop Up shops!

In bed at night we girls amused ourselves with a game we called: I know a Mary who goes down the Old Road. Now, the old road was the road that led from our gate to the town, and there were quite a few Marys living there, so the game was for the rest of us to try to guess which Mary we had in mind. We had to go through a process of elimination and were informed whether our questions were bringing us 'hot' or 'cold', closer or further away, in pursuit of the Mary in question. The successful identifier then got to select the next resident of choice on the old road or along one of the streets in town where we knew everybody – or if not, then this game soon introduced us to everybody. I have no idea where this game originated, but it kept us entertained most nights as we drifted off to sleep.

In town when we visited my aunt, we played Pickie with our cousins. For this game we used the squares of the pavement or else drew squares with a stone or chalk, which we sometimes stole off their father's desk as he was a teacher.

Into one square we placed a small stone and then, standing on one foot, we hopped along, kicking the stone ahead
of us. The aim was to get the stone into the centre of each
square with as few hops as possible. This game is also known
as Hopscotch.

On paper we played Fox and Goose. We drew squares by
pencil, and using noughts and crosses we tested our skills to
outdo each other in successfully completing straight rows
of noughts or crosses. Ludo and Snakes and Ladders were
the board games that we got at Christmas, and these were
brought out when the notion took us. Then we got a little
game called Pigs in Clover, which consisted of circles and
lots of tiny silver balls beneath glass. The aim was to get all
the little balls into the very small circle in the middle. This
was a solo game and very difficult, taking a long time to get
all the balls in. Often, when you were nearly there, you made
one false tilt and all the balls escaped and went rolling in all
directions. Then you had to start from scratch again. It was a
very frustrating game.

The swing hung off the branches of two large ash trees
in the grove. Two strong ropes held the little wooden seat in
position. If you wanted extra comfort you could put a bag of
hay on the seat. Sometimes we pushed each other very high,
but even on your own you got a good, high swing because
it was on an incline. You could walk backwards up the slope,
then sit on the seat and shoot out high over the valley below.

As you swung, you could twist the seat around and tangle the ropes, which gave you a great twirl. Once, owning to over-exuberant use, the rope broke and there was a crash landing. Our helpful neighbour, Bill, replaced the rope with iron horse traces. These were a great success as we could tangle the chains and do all kinds of somersaults, with no danger that they would ever break under pressure.

But one evening after milking, one of the cows happened to ramble into the grove on her way out to the fields, and as she made her way back to join the rest of the herd, somehow or other she got her front legs over the swing. The seat of the swing was now under her belly and the swing did what it was supposed to do, and swung her forward. Then back again in mid-air. As the cow lurched, the swing kept going. It was an extraordinary sight. If the rope had been still in use it would have broken and freed the cow, but the chain held fast. We thought it was hilarious to see a cow on our swing. But my father was not amused. Not a calm man in ordinary circumstances, he completely lost the cool this time, and all hell broke loose. The poor cow was addressed in unrepeatable language and Bill, though not present, was drowned in an uncomplimentary flow of adjectives. Cows by nature are not very excitable animals, but being on a swing was a new experience to this lady and she became a mad cow. And my father by now was a mad man. They made for a very explosive twosome. Plus, excited cows are apt to lose bowel control, and unfortunately my father happened to be in the direct line of fire, which did not improve the situation one bit. My brother, however, who thankfully had inherited my mother's tranquil nature, quietly got behind the cow and gave her a huge push. She lurched forward, dragging her hind legs behind her. The swing escaped from beneath her belly and she gave a high jump and landed safely back on solid ground. It was as near as we would ever come to seeing the cow jump over the moon.

Skipping was another challenging game; while one person skipped, another counted how many skips were taken. Sometimes skipping ropes came from Santa, or they might be bought in the local shop if budget constraints allowed. But often a length of binder twine left over from tying the hay wyndes did the job. The aim of this game was to outlast opponents. Sometimes a long farm rope was used, with a person standing and turning at each end, and the skipper had to gauge the rhythm of the rope when stepping into action – otherwise you could get a fine stinging wallop across the back of the legs, which could seriously limit your flexibility and reduce your chances of making a graceful high-step entrance.

Because we had few toys and no TV we had to fall back on our own resources to entertain ourselves. In later years when my own children, who were surrounded by toys, complained of boredom I informed them sternly that it

was only boring people who were ever bored. Now, as adults, they get great satisfaction in reminding me of my caustic comments.

Chapter 16

Minding the Bonhams

It is inconceivable in today's hygienic, health-and-safety obsessed world that pigs were actually brought into the family kitchen to deliver their *bonhams*. But before you snort in derision at such barbaric practices, take time to consider that in those tough economic years these animals were crucial to the survival of families. There was no social welfare and if you had no food you simply went hungry. On the farm, the animals were the food chain, so mother pig and her carers could not be left outside in a cold unheated pig sty to bring her valuable babies into the world. The survival of the young in the family home could depend on the future of these baby pigs. So the sow and her *bonhams* were the bank bonds of the time and could not be allowed to lose their value. They may not have smelt good, but at least they would not evaporate into thin air when bills were to be paid at the end of the year. But apart from the practicalities of survival, watching these animals and how our parents handled them also taught us children survival skills and animal care.

We have all heard the expression 'as ignorant as a pig' or 'pig ignorant'. But, whatever the source of that derogatory comment, it is totally incorrect and maligns the skilful thinking of a pig. Try to convince a pig to do something which she considers not to her advantage and you will soon discover who is the smartest. Her table manners may not be Downton Abbey standard, but her survival instincts are of mountain climbing calibre. And didn't she smartly stick to breast feeding when we humans decided that bottle was best? And now the human mothering world is rethinking the virtues of the natural food chain. Sometimes we have a lot to learn from the animal world …

Around the farmyard, Betsy, the sow, normally kept her head down and went about her own business. But this pattern changed when she was about to give birth. Her behaviour became agitated and erratic, and then it was best not to come into her line of fire. She prowled around the farmyard and haggard and up into the barn in an effort to find a comfortable corner to bed down and have her young. She pulled

bits of straw off the hay barn in an effort to make a birthing bed, but no sooner was she right than she was wrong again. Obviously labour pains kept her on the move and during this time my mother kept a supervisory eye on Betsy's behaviour. Finally my mother judged that it was time to bring Betsy into the birthing chamber, which was a small room off the kitchen. In here we usually kept our school coats and boots, buckets to feed the animals and a miscellaneous collection of farm tools. But all these had been evicted now and, after a scrub-out with Jeyes Fluid, one corner had been filled with soft straw. This was to be the labour ward.

Betsy, however, had other ideas and it took a human wall of hand-waving children and determined adults – some armed with various implements – to coax her in the door, but once Betsy sighted the straw she got the message and decided that this was not such a bad idea after all. She promptly began to make her bed, tearing the straw between her jaws and crubeens. When all was to her satisfaction she lay down, but no sooner was she down than she was up again, and resumed the same tearing routine. The night wore on and bed time approached, and no *bonhams* made their appearance, so it became obvious that a night nurse would be needed to act as midwife. Now, Betsy was well used to the challenges of delivery, having had several litters, but there was a slight flaw in her mothering nature in that when she went to lie down surrounded by her squealing offspring she was quite capable of lying on top of one of them and squashing it to death. This sounds as if Betsy was a heartless mother, but to be fair to her, over twenty babies in one go was enough to stretch the mothering capabilities of even the most ardent mother. But Betsy had yet another, and far greater, flaw in her make-up and that was if one of her young happened to outrage her beyond her endurance she would open her enormous snout and do a demolition job on the offender. This makes Betsy out to be cannibalistic, but we have to remember that Betsy's ancestors were wild boars who swallowed all before them in their struggle for survival, don't we? And so it was that, put under pressure, Betsy could go native – and some basic instinct warned me that if I got on the wrong side of Betsy I too could become part of her food chain, a sobering thought when she towered above you. Betsy was a bit like the zoo animals, who, no matter how tame and friendly they are with their keeper and trainers, are still wild animals and, like Betsy, can at any time revert to the original of the species.

Despite all these hazards, however, I had one great ambition when I was about seven years old and that was to stay up for a whole night minding the *bonhams*. My desire had absolutely nothing to do with caring for the baby pigs, but was a burning curiosity to see what the world was like in the middle of the night. Did the world smell different? Did it look different? What would it be like to have tea at night? What was it like with nobody around? I had seen the clock during the day at one and two and three o'clock and had often wondered what would it be like when the hands were back there again and it was the night time.

This was my chance! But as I was still very young I knew that it would take a certain amount of coaxing and brainwashing of my mother and the other carer to get what I wanted. There always had to be a second night nurse because it took two to adequately fulfil the job requirements. The first thing to ascertain was who was to be the head nurse, and when I discovered that it was a favourite sister, I set to work on her; once she was in my corner, my mother folded easily enough. I was going to be the trainee nurse!

I was delighted to see my mother, father, sisters and brother disappear up the stairs. Silence descended. I could hear the clock ticking. I had never heard it so clearly before because it was usually drowned out by the clamour in the kitchen. It was as if the heart of the house was beating. We stacked up the open fire and my sister settled down to read a book. I wandered around the house listening to the silence and looked out the window to see the night sky. Out there the trees were dark shadows and behind them the Kerry mountains were invisible; but I knew the mountains were there, hunkered down like silent monsters sleeping through the night. The moon was peeping through the branches of the big ash tree at the end of the yard. I would have liked to go out and walk around outside but I had listened to too many ghost stories about things that walked in the night. Then my sister and I decided to do some baking and we made an apple tart, planning to have it for our tea later.

My sister went to check on Betsy, who was remarkably quiet. But Betsy was actually busy with the business of delivery and two tiny *bonhams* had already slid effortlessly out from beneath her tail. My sister got a handful of soft hay and wiped the babies clean of the slimy afterbirth mucus, then she set them up against Betsy's ample bosom. They were a beautiful pale pink and soft as thistledown to touch. They knew instinctively what to do and wagged their little tails in delighted appreciation of Betsy's flow of sustenance. Subsequent babies slid into the world until a row of wagging tails lined up like a bank of pink snow against Betsy's giant supply tank. Once she got going, she gave birth with very little effort; all the stress and discomfort had been in the run-up. In the litter of twenty, there was one little weakling, which was known as an '*íochtar*', or the runt of the litter. He was too weak to win a position in the struggle with the stronger *bonhams* to gain access to Betsy's milk supply, so we transferred him to a butter box beside the fire and began to feed him with a bottle that my mother had left on standby. I loved doing this.

When Betsy was finished producing babies at around two o'clock we decided to have tea with toast and apple tart. I was delighted. This was what I had waited for. My sister swung the kettle over the fire and I began to make the toast. When all was in readiness we dined off a tray in front of the fire. It was a new experience for me and I loved it. I was all grown up!

After the tea I decided to lie back and relax for a few minutes on an old sofa beside the fire. Then the heat of the fire overcame me and I drifted off and when I woke up it was already four o'clock. I was mad! I felt cheated out of part of my night up. Then Betsy decided that it was time to stretch her legs and have a break from her demanding brood. She rose up, unceremoniously casting babies aside in all directions. We scooped them away with the kitchen brush from beneath her hard crubeens as she trod uncaringly though them. Out the door she sauntered and with her departure they all clustered together and promptly went off to sleep in a cluster of heads and tails.

Betsy's return was more problematic than her departure. She charged in, pulled the straw into her desired formation, irrespective of where her *bonhams* were, and threw herself down in the midst of them with more concern for the comfort of her bed than her young. Her young were *our* responsibility! So we grabbed them, squealing in protest, unceremoniously out of her way. As soon as she landed down like a giant whale, they all clustered around and she began a rhythmic feeding grunt which released a constant flow of milk into their demanding little snouts.

When the morning light began to creep in the window I decided that it was safe to go outside as all the ghouls of the night would more than likely have disappeared into nothingness. So I opened the front door and could hardly believe what lay outside. I stepped out into the golden wonder of the dawn. The trees around the house were edged with gold and behind them the sky poured a waterfall of colour down over the luminous mountains. It was breathtaking! And the dawn chorus filled the whole place with a symphony of sound. Minding the *bonhams* had its magic moments!

I Wandered Lonely as a Cloud
William Wordsworth

I wandered lonely as a cloud
That floats on high o'er vales and hills,
When all at once I saw a crowd,
A host of golden daffodils;
Beside the lake, beneath the trees,
Fluttering and dancing in the breeze.

Continuous as the stars that shine
and twinkle on the Milky Way,
They stretched in never-ending line
along the margin of a bay:
Ten thousand saw I at a glance,
tossing their heads in sprightly dance.

The waves beside them danced; but they
Out-did the sparkling waves in glee:
A poet could not but be gay,
in such a jocund company:
I gazed – and gazed – but little thought
what wealth the show to me had brought:

For oft, when on my couch I lie
In vacant or in pensive mood,
They flash upon that inward eye
Which is the bliss of solitude;
And then my heart with pleasure fills,
And dances with the daffodils.

Chapter 17

Tackling the Horse

Our horses had as many outfits as supermodels. They had an outfit for ploughing, another for mowing the hay, and yet another for going to the creamery. There was different tackling for every occasion in their life. The outfit for taking the trap to Mass on Sundays was top of the range, with highly polished leather and sparkling bits of brass edging. From there on down the job chain, it was more about solidity and durability than appearances and impressing the neighbours.

To tackle a horse you needed to know what you were doing and have a good knowledge of the various bits of tackling and the rudiments of how to get it all on the horse. You also needed to be confident and know your horse, because

if the horse sensed that you did not know what you were about, he could well decide not to cooperate. Then you were in big trouble! Like a bold child, he would kick and shake off what you had just put on, or even refuse to allow you to put it on in the first place by backing up and dancing around, so that he and the tackling never quite got into each other. The horse could well decide to do a quick-step around the yard and have you racing around after him. He could be merciless. I believe that to watch the wonderful footwork of a horse doing a fancy dance is to understand the rudiments of ballet or the high-flying footwork of Irish dancing – the horse was surely the forerunner of it all.

Horse tackling could be a complicated business, but essentially all tackling was made up of three elements: first, the parts for guiding the horse; second, the drawing piece; third, the parts for holding up the shafts and backing the vehicle.

When tackling a horse, the first thing to go on over his head was the winkers, which were the part of the tackling for guiding the horse, and consisted of a strap behind his ears, two cheek-pieces and a bit. The strap was firmly tied around his neck and the cheek-pieces were buckled to the bit, which went into the horse's mouth; the bit had a ring at either end to which the reins were attached. The reins were merely long narrow strips of leather or fine rope passing from the bit back through the hames and straddle loops to the driver's hand.

Next to go on was the drawing piece, which was a leather collar padded so as to fit comfortably around the horse's neck and shoulders. It was heavy, and it took a bit of manoeuvring to get it up around the horse's neck and tied firmly in place, before the horse decided to toss his head and side-step away from you. It was an achievement in time and motion, when horse and owner had to move in harmony to get the collar snugly in place. The padding of the collar was of horse hair, and it was covered over with pure wool blanket material. This material was warm and comforting to the touch and it fitted snugly on the horse's neck, preventing chafing from the heavy leather. The material was of the finest quality and cream in colour, with large red or blue stripes, and it came from one of the woollen mills that were all around the country at the time, which wove warm wool blankets used on the beds in every home – this was the era before the duvet crept into our beds and made these blankets redundant. Today the horses still wear pure wool and expensive top-class leather. In 1948 a horse collar in Days of Bowling Green Street in Cork, who were the top tackling shop of the time, cost two pounds and ten shillings, which was pretty expensive then. So horses were always in the best gear.

Around the collar went two iron bars with pointed ends, called the hames. The hames was buckled onto the collar by a strap at top and a chain at the bottom. When the chain at the base was secured, the hames strap at the top was tied by passing the straps through a flat eye and drawing the two irons tightly together. Towards the top of each hames was a ring intended to confine the reins in their place as they passed to the horse's head. The hames was a pretty awkward contraption, and the word even became part of our language: if you made a complete mess of something you would be told that you'd 'made a pure hames of it'. It was the ultimate put down!

The supporting and backing part of the tackling consisted of a heavy pad known as the straddle, somewhat similar to the riding saddle, but higher, narrower and lighter. This had two rings for the reins and a hook for the bearing rein, all at the top. It was fastened to the horse by a belly band and across it went a chain that attached it to the shafts of whatever they were pulling. Through the middle of the straddle passed a long leather strap, called the back band, which was attached to the breechen, which went over the horse's hind quarters and was also attached to the shafts. The breechen kept pressure back off the horse's hind quarters when they braked – the horses were very aware of this and paid close attention to its functioning.

The farm horses were multi-taskers, with many different jobs, from taking the trap to Sunday Mass, to going daily to the creamery, to cutting the corn and mowing the hay, to pulling the plough – all requiring a variation of the tackling theme. On certain occasions some pieces of tackling were dispensed with and on others extra bits were added, such as long traces for the ploughing and hay-making. But from constant use, each farmer knew instinctively how to tackle a horse for any occasion.

On our farm the tackling hung from the partition behind the horses' stable, which divided them off from the baby calves. Their stable was a stone, iron-roofed building in which the horses were separated from each other by timber rails to prevent anti-social behaviour, and they were over-seen by a chesty barn owl who hid in the rafters. A long manger ran along in front of their heads and hay was tossed into this in winter when access to the fields was limited. In the summer, like the cows, they grazed the farm fields, and one field was totally their domain and was named Páirc na gCapall (Horses' Field).

Because it was considered a cut above the other farm vehicles, the trap had its own house and its tackling hung in there beside it. Long, horse-hair filled cushions were placed along the trap seats, and these were sometimes carried into the kitchen on Saturday evenings to be aired, as my mother termed it, for the Sunday outing. And usually it was the pony who went to Mass while the horses were left to pray out in the fields and have a well-deserved day off.

Chapter 18

Fruits of the Earth

The Brake field, just inside the farm gate, was the best and largest field on our farm. It had rich dark earth – 'great arth', as my father called it. The Brake was a versatile field, which could be set aside for tillage, grazing or hay-making; one summer it was a meadow and when the hay was saved the cows grazed it, and the following spring it was ploughed for tillage. Each field on the farm had its own name and characteristics, and we had a working knowledge of them all. They were constantly walked, and short cuts were frequently taken across ditches to bring the animals back and forth. When some fields were set aside for hay-making, we spent hours walking around them as we raked the hay and made wynds that at the end of summer were drawn into the barn to feed the animals over winter.

Early on a February morning my father would pull the plough out of the dike and check that it was in working order, though in fact there was very little to go wrong with a plough. Then he tackled the horse to it and went around the headland to turn the first sod. That was the opening overture to an all-day performance. Ploughing the whole field was a mammoth task, but man and horse applied them-selves and for hours went up and down the long field. Clods of brown earth clung to my father's heavy leather boots, and the crows and gulls followed the plough to pick up the exposed worms. When we later brought tea out to him in the field we would always find him in a strangely meditative mood. It was as if during the long hours alone out there in the silence he found an inner peace. He was not ordinarily a patient or easy-going man, but when he was ploughing the fields he became so. Something in the ploughing of the earth soothed his soul.

We would wait for him at the bottom of the field until he finished the furrow he was doing. The furrows ran in long, wavy lines, following the lie of the land. As he drank his tea out of the white enamel jug and ate the brown bread we had brought, the horse grazed along the dike. It was good then to stand on the headland and view the even, brown furrows that contrasted with the green field, waiting to be penetrated by the plough and have its brown belly turned up to the sun, wind and rain. When the dusk fell, he came home and both he and the horse were earth-encrusted up to their knees. Sometimes winter ploughing took place in November and this gave the fresh furrows months to mellow beneath the winter weather.

After the day of ploughing, man and horse rested, and sometime later on a bright spring day, back they came, and the plough was replaced by a harrow. This was like a giant caterpillar with an underbelly of iron hooks that dug into the furrows and scrambled them into soft earth. It seemed a shame to upset the uniformity of the furrows, but some remained as they were to be used to set potatoes and other crops.

A few days later the corn drill came into action. This was a long wooden box and when you lifted up the cover you saw that it narrowed at the bottom where rows of little funnels ran out of it and down to the ground. Into this went the bags of seed and as the horse pulled the corn drill along, it discharged the seed down into the earth. Afterwards a long rolling stone was pulled over the seeded ground to settle them in and to partly hide them from the marauding crows. Sometimes a giant 'crow man' or scarecrow was erected to frighten them off, but the crows were often too smart for this trick. Now, all that man and horse could do was done, and the rest was up to God – but just in case he forgot, my mother reminded him with a sprinkling of holy water!

A few weeks later a faint sheen of green appeared through the brown earth and gradually grew tall and upright. Our crops were on their way. As they grew the difference between the wheat, oats and barley emerged and during the warm summer days they turned into different shades of golden yellow. The one danger to their success now was heavy rains or high winds that would cause the grain to lodge – this meant that it would fall sideways and besides making it very difficult to cut, it might rot. But if the summer was good it was in top form and ready to be cut in August.

Cutting the corn was a big day when a *meitheal* gathered from around the neighbourhood, and lined themselves all around the headlands ready to bind up the sheaves of corn once they were cut. My father sat on an additional seat that had been added to the mowing machine and from there divided the cut corn into the proper allotments for sheaves, while one of us guided the horses. Then the binders fell into place behind, and bound up the sheaves with strips of corn and tossed them sideways to make way for the return of the horses to cut the next sward. So it continued all day, with a break for food, until finally the entire field was cut and covered with bound sheaves that were then gathered up and built into stooks, where about a dozen sheaves stood upright supporting one another. A few days later these were built into tall stacks, and weeks later drawn by horse and float down into the haggard.

The next step was the threshing and this was the highlight of the farming year. The threshing machine coughed into the haggard the night before the threshing. It was a long, unwieldy, swaying wooden contraption dragged along by a puffing steam engine. It spent a long time spurting smoke and steam, and going backwards and forwards before the steam men were happy that the whole 'menagerie' was level enough to function properly.

Early the following morning the moan of the thresher brought the biggest *meitheal* of the year. Men carrying forks over their shoulders came across fields, down the boreen and over ditches, and poured into the haggard. There had been no need to notify anybody because the journey of the thresher around the farms was closely monitored, and once it was heard across the fields the *meitheal* gathered. As well as a work day, it was also a sociable gathering of the neighbours from the surrounding townlands. Because they had worked together for many threshings, there was no need for directions or instructions, as each man joined a group and began his own job. Some men uncapped the corn reek and tossed the sheaves onto the top of the thresher, while another group fed them down into the belly of the thresher, where it divided; the straw then came out the back end and men with pikes tossed it on to another group, who formed a straw reek. Chaff came out the side of the thresher to be cleared occasionally by another man, and the real yellow gold poured out the front of the machine. It was here at the front of the thresher that the main story of the harvest was told. The grain spilled out through narrow shoots into jute bags that were attached to each shoot. My father would catch the first grain in the palm of his hand and carefully examine it, then put it into his mouth and chew it, and when he nodded his head in satisfaction you knew that all was well. The harvest was good.

All day men drew the heavy bags into the grain loft where they poured it out onto the wooden floor, making sure to keep the wheat, oats and barley apart. The wheat would go to the mill to return to us as flour, the oats would feed the hens and horses, and the barley would go further afield.

Late in the evening, when the stack of grain was replaced by a reek of straw, and mounds of chaff littered the haggard, the drone of the thresher changed and she shuddered to a halt. The men scattered in all directions to go home to milk their cows. There was no need for thanks, as this would later be given in kind.

Then the engine men began the laborious job of manoeuvring the ungainly thresher out of the haggard. When she finally chugged her way slowly up our passage, we were sad to see her go. My father, however, breathed a sigh of relief as he strode across the haggard and opened the door of the loft that was now full of golden grain. He gave off an air of great satisfaction and so did my mother in the kitchen where she had fed the multitudes. Out in the haggard the geese, ducks and hens arrived in a flurry of ecstasy and dived into the chaff and loose straw, where they would have days of gourmet delight.

The land that fed us also fed our cows and horses, but sometimes some of these animals exceeded our requirements and had to be taken to the fair. Our town had two cattle fairs in the year and one horse fair. On the morning of the fair, cattle had to be rounded up in the early hours to be walked the three miles into the town. Here it was a case of the early bird catches the worm and often a good sale could be the result of being in the right place at the right time. Cattle job-bers, who were a wily lot, dressed in high leather boots and tan-coloured pants, were often out along the road to meet the early birds, and so the bargaining began. Offers, refusals, counter-offers could go on for hours, and often an interme-diary known as a 'tangler' came on board to help bridge the gap – and when the bargain was finally clinched with much hand-spitting and luck money negotiated, he had to get a back-hander.

A colourful crew of hangers-on came to the fairs too, more so to the horse fair. These included the three-card-trick man, whose fast-moving sleight of hand confused and fascinated young lads into parting with their money. Much drink was consumed and many a man had already drunk his morn-ing bargain when he staggered home in the evening. Long before the horse-fair day, the Travelling People were camped on approach roads, and on the day of the fair the women told fortunes while their menfolk traded in horses. Often, late at night, when sense and sensibility was long gone, a communal brawl brought the day to a rowdy end and the Guards sent them all on their merry way.

Trees

Joyce Kilmer

I think that I shall never see
A poem lovely as a tree.

A tree whose hungry mouth is prest
Against the earth's sweet flowing breast;

A tree that looks at God all day,
And lifts her leafy arms to pray;

A tree that may in Summer wear
A nest of robins in her hair;

Upon whose bosom snow has lain;
Who intimately lives with rain.

Poems are made by fools like me,
But only God can make a tree.

Chapter 19

Hear My Song

'If I was a blackbird I'd whistle and sing

And follow the ship that my true loved sailed in   '

Do you remember the words of the first song that you ever learnt? It is probably one of the things in life that you never quite forget. The first song that I learnt was 'If I Was a Blackbird', and the slow, sonorous tone of Delia Murphy made it possible to learn it off the radio. Our first aim was to learn the words, and the melody, or the 'air' as we called it, came later if you were lucky enough not to be tone deaf. But it was deemed very important to learn the complete words of a song. Delia Murphy had a very distinctive voice and in her rendering of the well-known song 'The

Spinning Wheel' you could almost hear the spinning wheel whirring beside you and visualise the old lady drifting off to sleep while still keeping half an ear to the goings on of a romantic minded young one. Delia increased the tempo in 'I'm a Rambler, I'm a Gambler', a great favourite with children.

My next venture into song was 'Way Down in the County Kerry', and in the rendering of this song a sprightly old couple called Kate and Pat Mc Gee stepped out in style (on a 78 record!) and danced to celebrate their golden jubilee! This was a rather odd choice for a twelve-year-old, but one that a sister who fancied herself as a bit of a musical director informed me I should learn as the dancing would cover up my lack of musical talent. We each had our party piece, but our brother Tim, who had a wonderful tenor voice, was always the star performer. He had a wide selection from 'The Lark in the Clear Air' to 'She Moved through the Fair'. One sister's party piece was 'Where the Shannon River Meets the Sea' and other sisters sang 'My Little Grey Home in the West', 'Galway Bay' and 'Loch Lomond'. My father, who did not have a musical note in his head, abstained from performance, but my mother's song was 'In a Tumbled Down Attic', which I never heard previously or since. One neighbour who was often present sang 'Far Away in Australia' and another performed 'My Mary of the Curling Hair'. Everyone had a favourite number – and if the necessity arose they

always had an encore at the ready. Impromptu home concerts would often take place and nobody wanted to be stuck
for a song. As for performance, the fact that you might not
be in harmony with the original composer was tolerated,
though not admired. We might not have been in Carnegie
Hall, but we were getting ready for it!

My most knowledgeable sister appointed herself as pre-
senter on these occasions. To prove how accomplished she
was as a concert impresario she liked to give little footnotes
to her audience in advance of a performance. Gentle persuasion was used to encourage reluctant visitors to come
forward, but where siblings were concerned her choice of
words was not of a delicate nature. Tact was not her strong
point and her introduction was delivered with a blunt instrument: before I made my appearance she invariably informed
the audience that the crow of the family was about to come
on stage! In later years I got great satisfaction in reminding
her of her lack of sensitivity and its longterm damage to my
musical self-esteem!

The magazine *Ireland's Own* was a great source of new
songs – one of us would learn the words and then teach it to
the others. Sometimes we learnt a song from the radio, and
when a song that we were endeavouring to learn came on
air there was an echoing shout around the house to round up
the potential Pavarottis. Each one of us picked up different
lines until finally we linked the whole thing together; it was

a case of joining the dots. If we had missing bits we filled in our own version until we learnt what the original composer had in mind.

In those days most people sang as they worked and milking the cows was the time when warblers tested their skills. The cow stalls were the practising pad for many potential performers and the bovine listeners were a tolerant audience. Young lads working with us on the farm had their own repertoire and often after supper played a melodeon or piano accordion as well. Others were into recitations and 'Famous Dan McGrew' often made an appearance in our kitchen in the evenings – I was always fascinated by 'the girl called Lou' who I figured was up to no good down at the back of the bar. Another recitation often recited was 'The Road Downhill', and I was intrigued by the oft-repeated line: 'the road downhill was an easy road and that was the road we went'.

The rendering of these recitations was usually given with a performance where the scene was acted out in our kitchen, different accents assumed and voice lowered and raised to produce the desired effect. These recitations were performed to an appreciative audience. Many of the favourites originated in Oregon in the USA, as emigration over the years brought songs and recitations back and forth across the Atlantic.

The gramophone was the greatest source of songs we learned. We would simply lift up the heavy 'horn' carrying the needle that ran around the grooves of the record, and set it back down again and again until we finally got a grip on the whole song, scratching many records in the process. This abuse of the records drove my father into a litany of complaints, so we waited until he was out of earshot and our learning curve would begin when his cap disappeared down the hilly field to the river. The preservation of his records was nothing compared to our thirst to be the next Vera Lynn, sweetheart of the forces, and to sing:

We'll meet again, don't know where, don't know when
But I know we'll meet again some sunny day.

Christmas was the time when new records were pur-chased. That was my father's job but no matter what he bought we were delighted, mainly because we had nothing against which to compare his choice. The gramophone was brought from the parlour into the kitchen for the twelve days of Christmas and it seldom fell silent. A new box of His Master's Voice brass needles kept it in voice and the wind-up handle restored flagging energy when the record slowed or worst of all faded away altogether. Over-winding was a disaster and could prove fatal or cause a gramophone heart attack, requiring major surgery. If the gramophone got such an attack we feared that our father could follow up with another one. But over the years we became adept gramophone handlers and treated it with the utmost respect. The records were kept in the deep drawer of the sideboard in the parlour, but over Christmas took their chances on the side table in the kitchen. These records were made from bakelite and were easily scratched and broken, so each record had its own jacket to avoid this happening. They were quite expensive by the standards of the time. John McCormack was the man of the day and he poured out 'Bless This House', 'The Fairy Tree', 'She Moved through the Fair' and many others. Another favourite was Fr Sydney McEwan, who sang 'Flowers of Fairest' to celebrate the Queen of the May. The powerful voice of Richard Tauber declared 'We re in love with you, my heart and I', while Joseph Locke gave a rousing performance of 'Goodbye from the White Horse Inn'. One of my favourites was the beautiful song 'Can I Forget You' and for the life of me I cannot now remember the name of the wonderful tenor who sang it. Maybe you remember?

Mario Lanza was another heart throb who invited us to 'Be My Love'. My mother's favourite was 'Cruising Down the River', and later 'Irene, Good Night' took over in her affections, and we waltzed around the kitchen to that one. We loved 'The Laughing Policeman', who laughed uproariously and whose laugh was so infectious that we just had to join in. We also had jigs, reels and hornpipes and, of course, waltzes. 'Over the Waves', 'The Blue Danube' and 'The Vilette' were favourites, but when one of my sisters tried to teach me how to waltz she informed me that I had three left legs!

The radio was a constant source of musical entertainment with programmes like 'Hospital's Requests' and 'Around the Fire', where Seán Ó Síocháin always got an attentive audience for his rendering of the song 'The Boys of Bár na Sráide'. The sponsored programmes played a wide variety of records that kept us up to date on musical trends. Here we were introduced to Harry Lauder, whose rich Scottish accent gave great gusto to his songs, and Guy Mitchell sang about an exotic female who 'Wore Red Feathers', and then he met 'One of the Roving Kind'. Of course, when Elvis came on air, he rocked our whole musical world – we were definitely moving away from Delia Murphy and her spinning wheel!

Chapter 20

Bring Blossoms
the Fairest

In our town, come midsummer, the procession took centre stage. There was no need to announce it or go over the details because everybody knew what the procession was all about. It was the Corpus Christi procession, which took place in early June, but because May had just made its exit it had a big spattering of that month incorporated into it. June was the month of the Sacred Heart, but May was his mother's month, and with the long tradition of the Irish Mammy there was no way she was going to be sidelined, so they both got even billing.

Because we did not live in town, flags and banners did not

flutter from our house. It was the one day of the year when I
wished we could have a house transplant. To be part of all the
fever of painting and decorating that preceded the procession was to me the height of excitement, and as my aunt did
live in town we became a mobile Mrs Mop team for her the
week before the big event. My mother was the Mrs Beeton
of the family, the wonderful cook, but unlike her townie
sister was not into 'house beautiful'. However, she was very
aware of her shortcomings in the housecleaning department
and so at every opportunity that presented itself she sent
her daughters to any local good housekeeping school that
became available – and my aunt ran the 'crème de la crème'
of such institutions. We became her clean team for the week
prior to Procession Sunday. We vigorously wielded Vim and
Ajax around her bathroom – and a bathroom to us was a
great novelty as we did not have one at home; we were still
making do with the tin bath in front of the kitchen fire or
a large bowl in the bedroom, or swimming in the river in
summer. So a bath that looked like a long white swimming
pool was an object of complete fascination. The only time
we saw such an abundance of water was in the river – to us
it seemed like an awful lot of water to wash just one person.
Of course, the reason we were cleaning the bathroom at all
when the procession only passed by the front door, was due
to my aunt's ingenuity in the utilisation of an available work
force!

When the inside of the house was scrubbed to perfection our hour came to really show off and we attacked the outside. It might have been painted the previous week by Paddy Bán, who was the local painter and decorator and meticulously stripped down all the sash windows and varnished the door with a final wobbly stroke known as graining. But if it was not the year for Paddy, we issued forth with buckets of water and brushes to wash down and prepare the way for the Lord to pass by the house. Once the scrubdown was done, it was window-cleaning time and here perfection was achieved with paraffin oil and newspapers until the glass was shimmering. After all, if the whole parish was to walk by, peering in as they went, we were not going to have Our Lady and the Sacred Heart inside unable to peer back out at them.

Then the night before the big event the real action that we had been waiting for began. Into the window to the right of the front door went a large statue of the Sacred Heart, and into the one on the left went a big picture of his mother. Around them went vases of flowers. At first the best vases came forth, but once we got to the upstairs windows we were often reduced to jam jars. Some houses did not do upstairs windows but our enthusiasm stretched above and beyond the bounds of normality. Up there the statue supply diminished to the lower orders, with St Theresa, St Bernadette and St Philomena – who, though we did not know it then, was an endangered species. Then a chipped St Patrick got an outing, and a dusty St Martin and a battered St Francis. These were representatives from the world stage of saints, so we could not be accused of being nationalistic or racist. Because we had never seen a black person, St Martin was a source of special wonder, and we concluded he must have come from a scorching hot country because no matter how long we stayed out in the sun we only made it to a deep brown.

Once all the windows were done, we paraded up and down in front of the house admiring our handiwork. Doing the windows was the dressing of the stage and now it was curtain-up time. All along the street men with ladders were erecting bunting across from one side to the other. There was no house across the street from my aunt's so we missed out on that bit of excitement, but we made up for it by helping the neighbours – at least that's what we thought we were doing, though the neighbours might have had another name for it. Some houses flew flags out the windows and any dodgy-looking area – like broken down gates or collapsed walls – had red and white, or blue and white material draped across them. There was a good face slapped on everything. The whole town was out and it was a case of all hands on deck! We had only one Protestant man living in town, and he was the local electrician and had long ladders, so he was roped in to help as well.

Arriving in the town on the morning of the procession was like arriving at a carnival, only far better and more festive. We were always early because we'd have badgered my mother into speeding up as we wanted to walk around and view the windows before Mass. We would see them all later on the procession around the town too, but that would only be a passing glimpse and we wanted to have a good long look. All these windows told a story. The pictures and statues of the house were in the windows and the flowers told the story of the garden behind. We looked forward to seeing Mike O'Brien's early roses and Maggie Jones's lovely lupins, and we remembered who had special pictures and ornamental statues. It was as if the interiors and gardens of the houses were peeping out through the windows and doors.

When my father had the pony and trap tied up safely in Denny Ben's backyard we headed for the church, but en route did a thorough inspection of windows. Some houses had open doorways too, with statues draped in veils at the entrance, and in order to get in and out people had to side-step around the arrangement. A windy day was a disaster as flower vases and statues took a tumble.

On procession day Mass was a bit of a prelude to the main event. We were eager to get out and get going.

A banner bearer, with two escorts holding the flying ribbons, lined up at the bottom of the church yard. He was the pace setter for the procession. A fast gallop was not desirable, but neither was a snail-paced crawl.

After a certain amount of confusion the children were sorted by the teachers into rows of four. You were dressed in your Sunday best and the little boys were in their nice new suits; if you were lucky enough to have got your First Holy Communion that year you had a special position further back. The women came next and then the men. Both men and women were heralded by banner bearers flying the flag of their confraternity guild. After them came the brass brand and after that the choir in full chant. Introducing a flash of blue and white came the Children of Mary in flowing blue cloaks and white veils, and then the First Holy Communion children, the girls delighted with the opportunity of this second outing in their lovely white dresses and veils. They carried little baskets of flower petals to be strewn on the ground in front of the Blessed Sacrament. Finally came the priests in flowing gold-embroidered vestments, and the robe of the main celebrant partly embraced the base of the monstrance that he was carrying under a richly embroidered canopy borne by four parish stalwarts.

Along the way the bearer of each confraternity emblem gave out the rosary and sang hymns with their own guild. But it was difficult to draw a line between where praying finished and singing began – and some people found it difficult to resist a chat with a neighbour, or a farmer might need to check the size of someone's creamery cheque. But,

all in all, a certain effort was made to observe the set procedure, even though sometimes singing and praying did get
mixed up.

Proper formation was supposed to take place in the church
yard, but it took the full length of the High Street, which led
down from the church, before any sense of law and order
began to set in. The plan was that all processed in rows of
four – but try telling that to an absent-minded woman who
ambled along, adding to and subtracting from rows as she
meandered. Or try straightening out a few young fellows
hell-bent on selecting the team for the next All-Ireland final.
It was the job of each confraternity leader to keep their flock
in order, but some flocks were less orderly than others.

After coming down High Street we turned the corner
into New Street and then back to the West End, where we
made a U-turn and then the procession doubled back on
itself and it was possible to spot some of our neighbours
and to see who had got a new hat for the procession. Then
back up New Street and left at the cross and there the two
Miss Gillmans, who sold smashing ice cream, would have
erected a wonderful blue May altar. Over the Scarteen Road
and another U-turn at the dispensary, and then left at the
Cross and along Church Street, so called because there, on a
raised green, was a gem of an old Protestant church, beside it
the graveyard where the bones of Sarah Curran, beloved of
Robert Emmet, rest. This little church was the jewel in the

crown of our town, later to be desecrated by the removal of its elegant steeple. We passed the barracks where four guards and a sergeant served and which had a glowing garden along the front. We would all note that the sergeant's wife had done a lovely job with the flowers and that the bank could have made a bigger effort – but, then, the manager's wife was not long in town so probably did not understand the importance of the procession! Then right again and in through the convent gate and up the long, winding tree-lined avenue to the impressive old building that was once the home of the Aldworth family, whose daughter, Lady Mary, was the only female member of the Freemasons. This was a male-only secret organisation, but having hidden in a wardrobe she was privy to one of their meetings, and when she was discovered there was no choice but to give her membership! Later, the building became the property of the St Joseph's order of nuns.

If we thought that we had the town looking good, it was nothing compared to the convent. At the top of the wide limestone steps that led up to the enormous front door was a high altar adorned with brass candelabra full of lit candles. Floating down over it from overhead windows were billowing chiffon drapes, which gave the impression of multi-coloured clouds pouring down from heaven. One year the candles set fire to the drapes when a breeze blew them in the wrong direction. The nuns were probably not too happy, but it certainly added to the drama of the occasion. We slowly formed a half-moon shape around the steps and overflowed back onto the front lawns. Then the priests under the canopy arrived and Benediction was celebrated from the high altar, the smell of incense from swinging thuribles filled the air and the choir chanted out the 'Tantum Ergo'. The Latin chants were beyond us, but once they launched into hymns like 'Hail Queen of Heaven' we were into familiar territory and sang at full volume, especially 'Faith of our Fathers'.

When the convent performance was over we headed back to our own church with a vague sense of anti-climax that was eased slightly as we passed the home of Rory Sheehan, whose front garden was always ablaze with roses that draped out over the wall. We would sniff them as we passed by. Back in our own church there were a few vacant seats as some people had decided that enough was enough and abandoned the procession before it ended. Then the band thundered up the aisle and disbanded in front of the altar, while the choir took over and sang us through another Benediction. When quietness descended the monstrance was placed on the altar and silent adoration known as the Quarantore began.

When we left the church we went to my aunt's house for tea and apple tart and afterwards did another tour of inspection of the town's windows. Then we all headed back to the pony and trap. The show was over for another year.

Years later when Frank Patterson sang 'Queen of the May'

he brought back the image of flying veils and fluttering petals and when Gay Byrne played it on his morning show it brought back many memories for me.

But we did not need to have all the elaborate trimmings of a procession to draw down blessings from above. On 'rogation days', which were the three days prior to the Ascension, and usually in May, my parents, having brought home Easter holy water, went out and blessed their own fields and crops. We walked along with them and afterwards I felt that our farm was holy ground. One evening I remember taking out tea to my father into a field where he had spent the day ploughing. As I went in the gap and looked across the furrows, I came to a standstill. The sun was sinking and he and his horses were silhouetted against the darkening skyline. I felt that I was looking at a sacred union of God, man and nature.

Chapter 21

Thank You,
Mr Cooper

Going to the pictures was the highlight of our
summer. The fact that we had a cinema in our
small town was a huge plus and, amazingly, it was a very
posh place, with gilded boxes and red plush seats. The boxes
curved out over the lower regions and were draped with red
velvet curtains. A wide staircase circled from downstairs to
the carpeted upstairs. My brother was a downstairs patron,
but my mother outlawed it for us girls. She was probably a
bit uneasy about what we might get up to in the shadowy
regions of the downstairs back seats. The cinema, as well as
being a rather grand place, also had a rather grand name:

The Casino. To my knowledge it never saw the roll of dice! Thomas G. Cooper of Killarney, a man ahead of his time, provided us and other places with The Casino, a name he gave to all his cinemas. He was the visionary who produced *The Dawn*, the first 'talkie' to be filmed in Ireland. As well as films, the Casino hosted concerts, plays and, wonders of wonders, rare dinner dances.

We were fair-weather patrons as we only went to the pictures in summer. It was not that the cinema closed down for the winter, but the prospect of walking the three miles back and forth in the rain and snow put a stop to our gallop. As well as that, my mother placed a curfew on winter outings; she had enough on her plate without adding lost children to her list of worries. Walking the hilly road home on a summer night did not cost us a thought. Often we sang along the road going into town, but on the road home our minds were full of what we had just seen, and we discussed and analysed it from every conceivable angle.

We loved the pictures and I became a huge film buff, haunting our local newspaper shop with my hard-earned pocket money, which I had got from thinning turnips and picking spuds. It paid for glossy film magazines and through them I became absorbed in the lives of the film stars. If Elizabeth Taylor sneezed in Hollywood, I heard it in north Cork. There were no paparazzi then, but a lot of details – true or untrue – were written about the stars. The beautiful Elizabeth became a child star in *National Velvet* and thereafter became the idol of the movie business. Her fairytale wedding to hotel magnate Nicky Hilton fascinated the world. I was her number one fan. Her subsequent husband replacements was a source of constant hope to me that one of them would finally fit the bill.

Our first picture in the Casino was *Maytime*, starring Jeanette MacDonald and Nelson Eddy. It was an unadulterated romance ideally suited to starry-eyed teenagers. Jeanette Mac Donald, draped in a wispy gauzy dress, reclined under an apple tree with showers of blossoms floating down on her. They fluttered to rest in exactly the right places while Nelson Eddy serenaded her from afar. As well as being handsome, he had the most wonderful singing voice, and this added wings to our unfettered imaginations. *Maytime* was undiluted fantasy without a shred of reality to blight the intoxication. And we loved it! Walking the hilly road home the night we saw it, we never even noticed the rocks or stones as we danced around in circles, thinking that we were Jeanette MacDonald. It was sheer escapism. The following day, after coming home from school, I took out my drawing book and tried to recapture the essence of Jeanette MacDonald and Nelson Eddy in watercolours. They would not have recognised themselves. I was not a portrait painter.

Hot on the heels of *Maytime*, Doris Day arrived on the Deadwood stage and high-kicked her way into the Casino.

She washed Jeanette and Nelson right out of our minds. Her energy levels almost shot the roof off our grand Casino. Her songs were catchy, vibrating with life and enthusiasm. Her gingham dresses swirled and bounced through hay-barns as she out-danced and out-sang her co-stars, Gordon MacRea and Howard Keel. We were entranced by *Seven Brides for Seven Brothers* and delighted by the antics of *Calamity Jane*.

Then came Barbara Hutton, who challenged Howard Keel – anything he could do she could do better. This song became an anthem in our house, where we used it to upstage each other when competing in different challenges. Running was one of the sports that brought out the most competitive streak in us, and sometimes on the way home from the meadow or walking along the road, a bright spark could get a sudden notion and shout 'race you to the next gate' – then we all took off like a flock of wild deer catapulted into a headlong race: it was a case of anything you can do I can do faster. *Annie Get Your Gun* also shot us into action.

Then the beautiful face of Ava Gardner came on screen in *Showboat* and sang 'Can't help loving that man of mine', and a whole new repertoire of songs came our way, including 'Old Man River' that really stretched our vocal chords. Then *The Quiet Man* brought us back home and we could not believe that John Wayne would drag Maureen O'Hara by her red hair across the fields. We thought that an actress could not come any more beautiful or breathtaking than Maureen – but then Marilyn Monroe appeared on our screen. She had something that drew all eyes in her direction. It was sex appeal, of course, though we had no name for that. Reading about all these stars in my glossy film magazines, I was fascinated to read in an interview with Jane Russell that when Marilyn complained to her about the treatment of the media, Jane Russell advised, 'Grin hard and bear it, honey, it's the price we pay for the money.' Some things never change!

It was in the Casino too that we first saw *Gone with the Wind* and marvelled at the outrageous Scarlett O'Hara, but identified with her conclusions at the end of the film when she declared 'Never sell land' and 'Tomorrow is another day'. Clark Gable, with his 'Frankly, I don't give a damn' we did not approve of, but we loved Norman Wisdom and listened to his 'Don't laugh at me 'cos I'm a fool' with great sympathy.

When the local drama group put on a concert or play, we were intrigued. This was local talent and though MGM was wonderful, it could not compete with seeing our own people on stage. Concerts were great, but a good play was riveting. To see locals dressed up in strange costumes at first challenged our imaginations to forget who they really were and see the characters of the play, but as we got caught up in the plot we soon forgot that the harridan on stage was actually the sober woman in the post office. In Bryan Mac-Mahon's *The Bugle in the Blood*, Mrs Monohan wailed 'What you suffered, what I suffered, what we all suffered ...' On the way home we rehearsed how we would say those words. Probably for that reason, we remembered these words long after the play itself was forgotten. In later years if any of us was acting the martyr, Mrs Monohan's words were recalled by a sister intent on bursting the bubble of self-pity.

One night before the curtain went up on a much-awaited performance, the very talented leading man spent too long in the pub. Before the producer came to grips with the situation and got him off stage, the leading man poked his head out between the curtains and announced to the amazed audience, 'I'm as drunk as an owl' and then disappeared. The audience, thinking that it was part of the performance, gave him a round of applause. An understudy was quickly summoned on stage.

All those years ago the Casino opened a door into the world of film and theatre in our small town. Thank you for the memories, Mr Cooper.

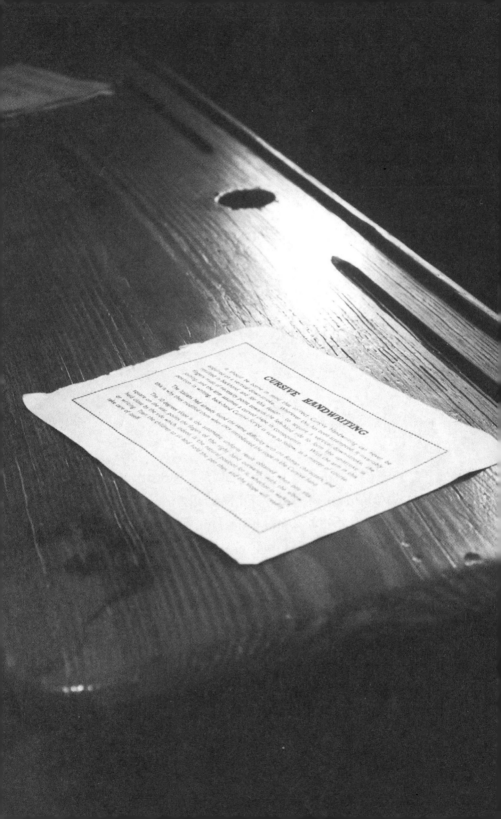

Chapter 22

Dancing with Eddie Fisher

Being very tall at a young age had its disadvantages. I was thirteen years old and too tall for my age which can make you feel all legs and hands, and awkward and insecure, a bit like a fast-growing plant that's unsure how to balance can easily fall over. Being tall had projected me forward faster than I could handle. It was my 'not fish nor flesh' period of not quite knowing if I was a child or an adult. It felt like a gap year between two worlds and I was unsure to which of them I belonged. I was a teenager, but 'teenagers' had yet to be christened!

A clutch of us had just stepped into secondary school and

were finding our feet in the challenging seas of many things, such as algebra and geometry. I was climbing a ladder where some of the steps were missing. Another problem was that when my brain was created, God forgot to insert the mathematical disc. English was my passion – I had a one-lane brain and that lane was English, overlaid with an active imagination. We had a brilliant English teacher, but, unfortunately, she had a tongue as abrasive as a rasp and was as intolerant as a wasp's nest.

One day I was in the front row of desks with six other girls. We did not have individual desks, but long church-like seating where about six of us fitted together like 'ten green bottles standing on a wall'. Because I was wearing a new, pale-green jumper, I was feeling particularly pleased with myself. New clothes were rare acquisitions. I was into film stars and going through my Debbie Reynolds period. I wanted to *be* Debbie Reynolds! Particularly Debbie Reynolds dancing with Eddie Fisher.

The desks across the room were filled with boys and the whole room was fertile ground for the sprouting green shoots of teenage hormones. For us girls, more important than impressing the boys with our brains was impressing them with our charm and beauty. And in my new green jumper I was out to impress one lad in particular who had red hair to match my jumper. I was sitting at the end of the desk and must have taken up what I considered to be a

Debbie Reynolds posture.

At the time you were given turns to read aloud to the class. One student began and at a moment's notice you could be pounced on to carry on. It was as much to check on your attention as your knowledge of the subject. Because I loved English I fancied myself as a good reader and loved reading aloud – I was probably a bit of an exhibitionist as well! That day, however, only my body was in the classroom. My mind was in faraway places. I was busy being Debbie Reynolds dancing with her new husband and co-star Eddie Fisher in their new film *Bundle of Joy*. I was totally oblivious to my surroundings.

Suddenly I was pounced on by my razor-tongued teacher. Blasted out of the *Bundle of Joy* I scrambled to my feet but had not the faintest idea where to pick up on the reading. A withering blizzard of sarcasm erupted from the top of the room. I got such a shock that my tongue clung to the roof of my mouth and my breath came in such short gasps that I could not breathe; I thought I was going to faint. After a further shower of belittlement I was told to sit down and not to be making an exhibition of myself. I sat down, shaking with fright, and feeling as if I had been ridden over by a herd of elephants wearing stilettos.

The following class was geography and the easy-going teacher called on me to read, but when I stood up no sound came out, only gasps. She looked at me in surprise and quietly told me to sit down. That night at home for the rosary I could not say my decade because I was so nervous.

It took me years to recover and I went to untoward lengths to avoid reading in public. At certain times the old fear reawakens. Childhood has a long memory. But despite that I still persist and mostly get away with it except when, like my grandmother, I am having a fragile day. But unlike her, I do not take to my bed. I go gardening instead.

So Eddie Fisher had a lot to answer for, and to think that he later danced off with Elizabeth Taylor and left poor Debbie Reynolds high and dry! So both Debbie Reynolds and I paid a high price for dancing with Eddie Fisher.

tá bó as

bíonn s

The Lake Isle of Innisfree

William Butler Yeats

I will arise and go now, and go to Innisfree,

And a small cabin build there, of clay and wattles made;

Nine bean rows will I have there, a hive for the honeybee,

And live alone in the bee-loud glade.

And I shall have some peace there, for peace comes dropping slow,

Dropping from the veils of the morning to where the cricket sings;

There midnight's all a-glimmer, and noon a purple glow,

And evening full of the linnet's wings.

I will arise and go now, for always night and day

I hear lake water lapping with low sounds by the shore;

While I stand on the roadway, or on the pavements gray,

I hear it in the deep heart's core

Chapter 23

Memories Are
Made of This

D o you remember your first dance? It may not have had the symbolism of being presented as a debutante in the marble halls of a gilded court, but it certainly marked a step from one world into another. We were finally waving goodbye to childhood and waltzing into a new, unexplored realm where the opposite sex suddenly became clothed in allure and the possibility of a romantic encounter added a certain lustre to life. Dances were where we took the first tentative step into the world of romance. But the first prerequisite to that experience was to master the art of dancing.

In our day, you did not venture into the unexplored territory of the dance hall without a certain amount of training, which meant that back home around the kitchen floor I was introduced to the waltz, quick-step, tango and samba. In grander circles mastering the intricacies of all these steps might have necessitated the skills of a good dancing teacher, but in our world older sisters took the task on board with unrestrained vigour and a certain lack of sensitivity. Another problem was a scarcity of suitable music as our gramophone records tended toward John McCormack, Richard Tauber and Joseph Locke. So when the notes of Victor Sylvester or Joe Loss pealed out from the radio there was an immediate call to arms for this would-be ballroom dancer. I was unceremoniously hauled around the kitchen, accompanied by a flow of derogatory remarks about two left feet. After much practice, I finally mastered the art of channelling the rhythm that was in my head down into my feet. Finally I was deemed ready to be launched.

Our local dance hall, known as the Stella, did not exactly have the special floor and arched ceiling of a grand hotel ballroom. It was actually part of the local garage, with petrol pumps to the front and a working garage underneath, so the smell of oil and petrol added a certain explosive atmosphere to proceedings. In today's world it would without question be declared a health and safety hazard and a closed sign would be slapped across it before it even opened its doors.

However, the low ceiling and crystal ball that immersed us in exotic flashing lights was magic to us. It had its own resident band called The Roy Campbell, and they filled the hall with the vibrant sound of a saxophone, piano, drum and a piano accordion. They had two singers, one for the slow, smoochy numbers and one for the rollicking rock 'n' roll ones. Nobody stayed seated by choice when The Roy Campbell struck up. Being partnered by a good dancer was a great plus because having a partner who did not know what to do with their feet put a damper on the rhythm. If the crowd were slow to get moving the band struck up a 'Paul Jones', where everyone got to their feet and marched around the hall and you partnered whoever was standing in front of you when the music stopped. It was a real lucky dip! The next motivator to movement was the Siege of Ennis or a Ladies' Choice – which proved that the ladies could get things moving faster than the men. Whoever you picked for Ladies' Choice was really getting a sign of approval.

The summer carnival dances were the launching pad for us teenagers who had just done our Inter Cert, which was the educational high jump of the time that you cleared at about sixteen. Then you were ready to savour other aspects of life. You were not a solo runner, because every girl in your school year was similarly engaged. The boys were also making their debut, but we deemed that they did not feel the same sense of excitement.

The dance was on a Sunday night and after Mass friends gathered and all that day was spent in preparation. You were never quite sure what dress was going to be yours until all the fitting on and preening in front of inadequate mirrors was done. We fitted on and changed into each other's dresses until finally a decision was reached on what showed each one of us off to the best advantage. Dresses had been washed and sometimes starched the previous day and then ironed that morning. Billowing petticoats, some made of stiff tulle, gave skirts the desired swirling effect. We all wanted to be Doris Day! And it had as much to do with impressing each other as attracting potential suitors.

At the end of our fashion parade, I finished up for my first dance in a white dress strewn with pink roses that reached far below my knees – skirts up as far as possible and tops down as far as possible were away over a distant horizon. It had a tiny stand-up collar and puff sleeves. I was like Little Bo Peep without the sheep. But I thought I was gorgeous! Hair was washed, curled, brushed up, brushed down and arranged into all kinds of angles until finally it was deemed right. It was the era of the steel curling rollers and often the hair was saturated the previous night in messy setting lotion and then rolled around these crucifying curlers – and you went to bed with a head wrapped in an uncomfortable iron helmet. All just to add body to lifeless locks. How we suffered to be beautiful!

Once we were dressed to our satisfaction, we moved up into the facial zone. Fresh young skin was obliterated under pancake make-up and gaudy lipstick liberally applied to lips. When my lipstick was inspected by an older sister I got a quick wipe of a tea towel. I was giving the wrong impression she informed me, and my reputation had to be preserved.

We walked the three miles into the town to the dance and home again afterwards, so shoes had to be suitable for walking as well as dancing. Thus there was no possibility of tottering around in six-inch heels. If you felt the need of anything more elegant than a walking pair of shoes, you had to carry them in a parcel under your arm.

Arriving in the carnival field you did a walk-about to display your elegance and impress the neighbours. The big spinner, the pongo and the swinging boats, that in previous years had been a source of high excitement, had now paled into boring territory. In those pre-dancing years, the sound of the music that began to emit from the Stella as we left the field to walk home in the semi-darkness, was simply a source of idle curiosity. Now, however, it vibrated with our teenage hormones, and we were ready to dance. We lined up outside the ticket box, paid up and trooped in. The pulsating music hit us like a tornado and we became immersed in a sway of bodies around the entrance. On my first night a friend dragged me to the ladies' cloakroom where girls were dabbing on lipstick and blinding each other in clouds of perfume and hair spray. We escaped back out into the hall and looked around breathlessly at couples swirling around us. This was a foreign land! How would we cope and survive? Thankfully, male schoolfriends and neighbours, who, in previous weeks, had often been a source of irritation now turned into knights in shining armour. I discovered that trying to dance around a sticky kitchen floor bore no resemblance to gliding around this wonderland that dancing crystals had turned into a skating rink. Fellow students, who were dull as ditch-water in class, had suddenly developed into dream waltzers. It was amazing the transformation that atmosphere and music could achieve! Soon we got a grip on dancehall strategy and, as potential partners lined up across the hall, we learned to strategically place ourselves in the line of vision of a desired partner. But sometimes this did not work and someone tapped you on the shoulder and you found yourself looking into the face of an undesirable experience. There was always the excuse of 'I'm already asked' which could be true, but was sometimes used to get us out of a tight corner if a whiff of alcohol or something else undesirable offended your sensibilities. Older friends and sisters had already filled you in on the ground rules.

The dance began at ten o'clock and went on until three in the morning, and it was a learning curve. At one stage I found myself dancing to my delight with a handsome, lively young man, and when he returned for another dance new thrills went up and down my spine. They were short-lived however, as an older sister whispered in my ear, 'Keep away from him, he's up to no good.' That knocked some of the stars out of my eyes. I didn't know exactly what he was up to, but I knew better than to argue with my chaperone. My dashing Romeo had feet of clay and I was as chaperoned as Eliza Doolittle.

I used the strategy of tactfully avoiding my pursuing suitor and soon recovered my equilibrium to discover that simply dancing for the sheer delight of it had a lot to recommend it. After the dance we walked home in a group and discussed all the happenings of the night. The preparations and the post-match analysis were almost as good as the dance itself.

Shortly after this the showband scene took off, and dance halls became bigger and better. Crowds flocked to these huge venues and Ireland danced to the sound of the Clipper Carlton, Dickie Rock and the Miami, Joe Dolan and the Drifters, and Brendan Boyer and the Big 8. The lead singers became pop stars and the ballroom owners became million-aires, and for the first time in Ireland since the famous boxer Jack Doyle, we had celebrities. Excited girls in a flurry of exultation threw bras and knickers onto the stage at the feet of Dickie Rock, and expressions like 'Spit on me, Dickie' made shocking reading for parents who assumed that in no way could that be their daughter.

Then Elvis Presley donned a pair of blue suede shoes and

teenagers began wriggling their hips in what most parents judged to be a most unseemly fashion, and Radio Luxembourg became the channel of choice for all young music lovers. Later the soothing voice of Jim Reeves invited the romantic minded to 'Put your sweet lips a little closer to the phone', and continued to hypnotise the starry-eyed with 'Magic Moments', which caused many a bewitched dancer to answer yes when they actually meant to say no. Then four long-haired young men from Liverpool introduced Beatlemania and teenyboppers lowered the age limit for musical hysteria. But at the same time, in hidden corners of rural Ireland, céilí bands such as the Gallowglass and the Kilfenora kept Irish traditional dance music alive.

Different phases come and go, but music and dancing go on forever, and eventually record-playing discos came on the scene and the DJ's became the new celebrities. But no matter who provides the music most of us remember the tune we danced to when we first met the special person in our lives. It becomes 'our song'. The sound of that tune forever afterwards brings back happy memories, and in our house when our tune was played we dropped everything and waltzed around the kitchen to 'Memories Are Made of This'.